CW01246360

WHO'S WHO GUIDE TO

Protocol

David Ford

INFORMATION AUSTRALIA

Published by
Crown Content Pty Ltd
A.C.N. 096 393 636
A.B.N. 37 096 393 636
75 Flinders Lane
Melbourne Vic. 3000
Telephone: (03) 9654 2800
Fax: (03) 9650 5261
Internet: www.infoaust.com
Email: mail@infoaust.com

Copyright © 2001 David Ford

All rights reserved. This publication is copyright and may not be resold or reproduced in any manner (except excerpts thereof for bona fide study purposes in accordance with the Copyright Act) without the prior consent of the Publisher.

Every effort has been made to ensure that this book is free from error or omissions. However, the Publisher, the Authors, the Editor, or their respective employees or agents, shall not accept responsibility for injury, loss or damage occasioned to any person acting or refraining from action as a result of material in this book whether or not such injury, loss or damage is in any way due to any negligent act or omission, breach of duty or default on the part of the Publisher, the Authors, the Editor, or their respective employees or agents.

The National Library of Australia
Cataloguing-in-Publication entry:

Ford, David, 1938-.
  Who's who guide to protocol.

  ISBN 1 86350 366 8

  1. Diplomatic etiquette. 2. Diplomatic etiquette - Australia. I. Title. II. Title : Guide to protocol.

327.2

Cover & Page Design: Ben Graham

Printed in Australia by Brown Prior Anderson

Dedicated to all who worked with me over many years. No one could have asked for a more loyal, dedicated and professional group of work colleagues. They saved me on innumerable occasions and I am indebted to them for their unfailing support.

ACKNOWLEDGMENTS

In the preparation of this book I was enthusiastically supported by many colleagues from the protocol organisations in the States and Territories. They offered advice on the content and guided me on specific matters where detailed arrangements differ slightly between the various jurisdictions.

I would especially like to thank, in no particular order, Pat Vaughan from the Department of the Prime Minister and Cabinet and my state and territory colleagues, Cliff Lonsdale LVO OAM from NSW, Graeme Roberts-Thomson MVO RFD from Queensland, Dale Keady MVO from WA, Cuijeta Ahwan MVO from SA, Fiona Birkett MVO from Tasmania, Peter Farrell from NT and Christine Chatillon from the ACT.

My special thanks also go to all members of the protocol organisation in Victoria but especially Paul Morrison MVO and Alexandra Karadaglis who read the drafts and did not spare themselves in offering constructive comments.

I am indebted to the Honours Secretariat at Government House, Canberra especially the Director, Amanda O'Rourke for the generous assistance I received.

To the many others who assisted me, but have not been named, my heartfelt thanks.

Contents

Introduction vii

Chapter

1	Visitors	1
2	Hospitality	23
3	Ceremonial Matters	71
4	Honours and Awards	107
5	Symbols	127
6	Other Matters	143

Appendix

A	Australian Protocol Offices	154
B	Visiting Dignitary Check List	158
C	Hospitality Check List	166
D	Formal Replies to Invitations	170
E	Forms of Address	172
F	Official Commonwealth And State Symbols	178
G	Australian Government Information Shops	180
H	Australian National Anthem	182

Introduction

The word *protocol* has a number of dictionary meanings but basically they all boil down to a set of arrangements acceptable to a number of parties. This can be in the diplomatic or etiquette sense. This book deals mainly with the etiquette or everyday meaning of the word. How do we apply protocol in our everyday lives to enhance our success in the business or social world?

Protocol is often regarded as something of a 'black box' in which there is a group of experts in such matters who can be approached when help is needed. This is not the case. We consider protocol matters in our everyday business dealings with clients and potential customers. We consider it when organising a social function, be it a formal dinner party or a backyard barbecue (although the latter may require a little less thought). We apply social rules and guidelines every day without consciously thinking about them. For example, there would not be many people who would attend a relative's funeral wearing a T-shirt, shorts and thongs.

Protocol is often thought of as being stuffy and formal - made up of rules which do not change. Nothing could be further from the truth. Protocol is dynamic but not in a revolutionary sense. The change is evolutionary but change there certainly is. When preparing for the visit by The Queen in 2000, the programmes from the last visit 10 years previously were perused. This exercise showed just how much change there had been. The perception of the Royal Family had changed and how things were done had changed. We had a good chuckle at some of the activities that had been so successful 10 years before.

People often speak about protocol rules. It is better to think of protocol guidelines rather than rules. Guidelines have that essential element of flexibility which allows them to be applied effectively to precise and specific events and occasions. I have always refused to answer hypothetical questions on whether something should be done this way or that way. You need to know the purpose of the event, what is hoped to be achieved, who is attending, the time of day or night and a host of other matters which will guide you, within a set of guidelines, to determine the most effective protocol for this specific occasion. There is rarely only one way of doing something. There is always a most effective way of doing it.

You will find that this book is full of guidelines and not many rules. In many cases matters are not prescribed, but there is a general discussion and a reference to where current and detailed information may be obtained. This is because of the dynamic nature of some protocol matters and some subtle differences in the application of general guidelines by the Commonwealth, States and Territories.

If you hope to find details in this book of how to plan and conduct a Royal or Head of State visit, you will be disappointed. There are only about 20 people in Australia who will ever have to do this. They are the protocol professionals who have this knowledge and wide experience in such matters. These colleagues will be my greatest critics! This book is not for them.

If you are looking for details on how to address the Grand Pasha of Lower Turkmenistan, you will also be disappointed. It is not a book of extreme and obscure detail. The book is designed to help those people who brush up against formal or official occasions from time to time or are called on to organise such activities and want a little confidence-boosting knowledge and guidance.

The contents of the book could be regarded as rather basic by some readers. This may be so but it is based on the questions that I and my colleagues in the State protocol offices are asked every day by members of the community.

There are already some reference books on protocol matters available in Australia. However, most of them are dated or do not relate to Australian practice. Additionally, they are specialised in their application. For example, there are a number of books available on weddings and the naming of children. You will find no such references in this book!

Protocol really relates to courtesies and arrangements which make all those involved feel relaxed and comfortable. It is the application of plans and procedures which lead to that result. Good protocol is made up of 70% commonsense, 20% knowledge of some simple guidelines and 10% good luck.

Throughout this book I have used the word 'States' when referring to the States and Territories of Australia. This is for simplicity and to avoid a tedious syntax. References to the Governors of the States include the Administrator of the Northern Territory unless specifically excluded. On the matter of gender, this has been alternated chapter by chapter.

The book has been generally written from an official or business application rather than from a social viewpoint, except where it is important to highlight the differences. The term 'spouses' has been used to encompass wives/husbands/partners/friends, except where there is a specific need to separate the categories. Full stops are now not generally used after abbreviations or post-nominal initials and this style has been followed throughout the book.

I hope you enjoy the exploded 'black box'.

* * *

When I started my appointment as Chief of Protocol with the Victorian Government, an ambassador advised me that I would have three problems during my career. They would be Protocol, Alcohol and Cholesterol.

He was not far wrong!

Chapter 1

Visitors

VISITING DIGNITARIES

Visits by anyone can be important for the business, organisation or group concerned. Unfortunately, the arrangements often receive less than proper attention. The purpose of the visit should be carefully considered. The programme should then be tailored to maximise the success of your aims as the host, but you must also consider the aims of the visitor. These may not be the same.

This section is based on visits by senior dignitaries. It could be the Prime Minister or the Premier, it could be an important business visitor where you are in competition with others for a contract, or it may be a visit by your overseas-based company chairman. Although the guidelines are based at this level, they are generally applicable to any important visitor.

It is often difficult to get senior management to focus on a visit by a dignitary some weeks in advance, but this is the critical time to establish the outcomes required so those who are responsible for making the arrangements have a very clear view of what is required. You can contrast this with a visit overseas by senior management themselves where they are very interested in the quality of their programme at an early stage of the planning process. This particularly applies within government where Ministers generally take very little interest in receiving calls from visitors but are very anxious to make meaningful calls at the highest level when they travel!

Once the aims and desired outcomes are decided from the host's point of view, it is necessary to find out the aims of the visitor. This can sometimes be difficult but is important for the visit to be successful. If the aims coincide, the visit is almost guaranteed to be successful but there is normally some compromise needed.

With the aims decided, the development of the programme can begin. The key elements of any programme development are:

- Keep the aims and outcomes clear. Logistics must bend to make the strategic or policy aims work.
- Continuing communication with all who are concerned with the programme. This means communication in every sense of the word - telephone, facsimile, e-mail, distributing copies of draft programmes and personal meetings. The regular distribution of the draft programme as it develops is the best method. People see the whole picture. Draft programmes are very helpful in keeping senior management informed and involved.
- Reconnaissance or rehearsal. People will often agree to a proposed procedure when it is described to them but, in their mind, they may be visualising something completely different to you. Standing on the ground and then walking through the arrangements ensures that everyone knows what is proposed. Reconnaissance can be time-consuming but remember the old adage: *Time spent in reconnaissance is seldom if ever wasted.*

- Develop sensible logistic arrangements to support the programme. Keep the standard of arrangements appropriate to the level of the visitor. Look for one or two small initiatives which will lift the visit beyond the standard - for example, a short personal note of welcome from the host and a small gift in the hotel room on arrival.
- Apply commonsense throughout. Make sure all the arrangements are courteous. Avoid any awkward or contrived situations.

A visiting dignitary checklist is attached at Appendix B.

If you are inviting a person or delegation to visit as your guest for a day or so, it is essential to establish in the invitation papers exactly what you mean by 'as our guest'. The guest's assumptions of this rather general phrase may be somewhat different from what you have in mind. Do you mean that you will meet the cost of airfares, accommodation (including all meals, mini-bar, laundry and telephone calls), ground transport and entertainment? What about medical and possibly hospital costs? If there are 10 people in the travelling party, will you look after them all or just the principal visitor and two support staff? These arrangements should be clarified right at the beginning so that there are no nasty surprises at the end which may sour an otherwise successful visit. A list of what you will do, attached to the formal invitation letter, is the best way to go. It is then clear to the guest what is proposed before the invitation is accepted.

Some overseas visitors may be concerned about personal security. They may not be aware of the comparatively secure environment which applies throughout Australia. The various police services may provide a police security presence if the visitor is an Internationally Protected Person (basically this only applies to certain political office holders or government appointees) or there is a positive security threat established through the various police intelligence agencies. They will not normally respond to a request for security support because the visitor feels that he or she should have (or would like) some security cover. If personal security is an important element in the visit planning you should raise the matter with the appropriate police service. They may advise you to engage a private security agency for this purpose. You must also advise the appropriate police service if the visitor intends to be accompanied by his own personal security officers. There are very strict regulations throughout Australia covering the actions and jurisdiction of any foreign security officers who are not registered with the Australian police services.

Gifts and briefing papers/handouts need some consideration, particularly with overseas visitors. Most visitors travel in commercial aircraft and have a baggage limit like the rest of us. The last thing they need is to be presented with a mass of weighty documents and a heavy or bulky gift on the last day of their visit just after they have managed to cram their personal belongings and some gifts for their family into their bulging luggage. This is an invitation for the papers to be dumped in the airport rubbish bins! Gifts should be kept small and as light as possible. Large coffee table books are not particularly suitable, nor is a presentation six pack of Australian wines or a child-sized stuffed koala. There may be important background or briefing papers that should travel. Make the offer to freight the bulky papers or gift to the visitor's home office. The six pack of wine arriving a few days after the visitor returns home may have more impact than a face-to-face presentation. These are courtesies that are sure to be appreciated.

Hosts need to be aware of the cultural differences that may exist with some visitors. Although the amount of travelling undertaken today has tended to create a more understanding and global citizen, there are still some special courtesies that should be followed. Some religions have restrictions on food and drink; other nationalities have superstitions on colours or numbers or particular days of the week.

Asking the visitor's staff during the preparatory stage whether there are any particular matters to consider will not always bring forth a useful response. You should consider seeking advice from other sources such as the appropriate chamber of commerce and industry, the local consulate or from the Department of Foreign Affairs and Trade in your State. Sometimes, the differences appear very out of touch with standards applied in Australia but to ignore them can affect the result of the visit. For example, one visitor from a strongly Islamic country refused to speak to the female escort officer who had done all the visit preparation work. A male escort officer had to be found very quickly.

News media may accompany a visitor, especially if the visitor is a high-level politician. Their handling requires some consideration. A dozen or more media representatives running out of control can spoil the visit.

You also need to consider any 'in-house' photographers that you wish to employ to have a pictorial record of the visit for your own use. Do not rely on the general news media - they will not necessarily be taking the types of shots you want to use in your annual report or other publications. You should consider the following:

- There may be still photographers, TV crews and journalists. The visual recorders require the most attention. Unless they are given locations to get good shots, the pictures will not be used. This is to no one's advantage.
- Media representatives are not noted for standing passively in a poor position. They will go to where they consider is the best location, which may upset previously made arrangements. If you are not conversant with their requirements, seek the advice of your in-house media relations staff.
- Keep in mind the outcomes of the visit that you want and try to arrange media locations to support these aims. Action shots

with some human interest are best. The media are generally not enthusiastic about 'talking heads', although there should be arrangements for speeches to be covered. Unless there is something really important or controversial said, they are rarely used. Analyse a couple of evening television news presentations and look at photographs that appear in the newspapers - they will give you an idea of the visual material that is likely to be used.

- All media should be given the same opportunity. To have the general news media in one location and your in-house photographer or a specialised (or favoured) photographer in another with special privileges will immediately create a conflict.

- In restricted locations such as a small room, it may not be possible for all media to be present. The news media may agree to 'pooling' in such circumstances. This is an agreement where one TV crew will cover the activity and make its video available to all other media outlets. They then add their own audio comments on the video elements they select. Similar arrangements apply to still photographers and journalists. Such arrangements will be resisted strongly and negotiations with the attending media need to start early (certainly not on the day). The negotiations should be conducted by a person who can talk in news media language.

- The appointment of an officer to brief the media and control/guide their movement is almost always necessary. A media briefing document handed out on the day will help to ensure names are correctly spelled and will give you an opportunity to focus the news media attention towards the important outcomes you want to achieve. Make it user-friendly - avoid complicated or highly technical language which will be a turn-off for all but the specialised media. If the technical aspects are important, add a technical annex to a more general brief.

The form of the working programme can add to the success of the visit. Everyone likes to see their name in print and to feel that something special has been done for them. In preparing the physical programme document the following should be considered:

- A hard-cover programme that does not fit into a pocket or handbag, no matter how stunning the cover design may be, is not particularly useful.
- A visit programme should be just that. It should not contain extensive background or briefing notes. If required, they should be separate.
- A programme printed on A4 paper clipped in the top left-hand corner which can be folded to fit in a pocket is a basic-level programme. A programme around A6 size with a light card cover, printed in colour and bound, shows that some special effort has been made for this visit. Such programmes can be produced quite easily through a range of computer programmes now readily available.
- The content of the programme should show times, places, activities and personalities who will meet.

An example is shown below.

COMPANY LOGO

VISIT TO
GRANADATECH PTY LTD

BY

THE HONOURABLE JOSEPH BALDWIN
MINISTER FOR DEVELOPMENT

IN THE
GOVERNMENT OF LOWER MOROVIA

*

WEDNESDAY 25 - FRIDAY 27 NOVEMBER

WORKING PROGRAMME

THURSDAY 26 NOVEMBER

0840   Meet John Taylor, Escort Officer, in the hotel lobby adjacent to the concierge desk.

<u>MEET WITH THE CHAIRMAN, GRANADATECH</u>
0850   Leave for the city office of Granadatech, 146 Smith Street, City by car.

0900   Arrive. Proceed by elevator to level 12. Met by:

        Mr Harold Jones, AO
        Chairman, Granadatech Pty Ltd

In the boardroom Mr Jones introduces the other members of the Board (See pink pages at the rear of this programme for names and appointments)

Discussions on the Manhattan Project.

1030   Morning tea.

1130   Discussions conclude.

<u>VISIT TO THE OAKVILLE MANUFACTURING PLANT</u>
1145   Leave for the Granadatech manufacturing facility at 36 Grand Street, Oakville by car, accompanied by Mr Terry Walsh, Managing Director, Granadatech Pty Ltd.

> **THURSDAY 26 NOVEMBER**
>
> 1215 Arrive. In the main lobby met by:
>
> > Mr Tim Sullivan
> > Plant Manager
>
> Mr Sullivan introduces his key staff members.
>
> Proceed to the dining room for lunch.
>
> 1230 Two course lunch is served
>
> **PLANT INSPECTION**
> 1345 In the annex to the dining room don protective overalls.
>
> 1350 Escorted by Mr Sullivan, proceed to the Technology Design Unit on Level 1. Observe planning for the Manhattan Project. Speak to staff.
>
> 1415 Proceed to the Equipment Validation Section on Level 1. See technical work in progress. Meet Dr Jane Bartram, exchange scientist from Lower Morovia.
>
> 1445 Proceed to the main manufacturing line on the ground floor. See manufacturing and preliminary testing activities. Speak to staff.
>
> *Etc, Etc*

For Further Information:

- Contact the appropriate protocol office listed in Appendix A.
- Although aimed at American business relations, the book *Kiss, Bow or Shake Hands* has some useful information on country backgrounds, customs, cultural orientation, protocol and gift-giving. It was published by Adams Media Corporation in 1994 and is available in many community libraries.

* * *

During the visit by the Irish Prime Minister, Charlie Haughey, his programme included a visit to St Patrick's Cathedral. At that time there was a very active Irishman living in Melbourne who spent much of his time standing on the steps of the GPO at the corner of Elizabeth and Bourke Streets addressing passers-by on all manner of topics. These varied from what was wrong with governments (all of them) to the inequities of Collingwood losing their game on the previous weekend. Unbeknown to us he had some strong views on Charlie Haughey and what he was doing for the Irish people. He established himself on the footpath outside St Pats and, armed with a quite powerful loud hailer, began to broadcast his somewhat uncomplimentary views in rather colourful language to the visiting party inside the cathedral. The Dean of the Cathedral became very agitated at the comments and, armed with his walking stick, proceeded out of the Cathedral to deal with the matter. He crossed the Cathedral forecourt, obviously had an animated conversation with the Irishman, complete with much waving of the walking stick, and then returned to the visiting party just as they emerged from the front door of the Cathedral. As he did so, this amplified powerful Irish voice rang out: "Well Ladies and Gentleman. Would you believe this? A servant of God just told me to bugger off."

ROYALTY AND VICE-REGAL REPRESENTATION

There was much debate in Australia regarding our constitutional form of government during 1999/2000. The debate is likely to continue. Without getting into the constitutional or legal details, the basic arrangement is that Australia's Head of State is Queen Elizabeth II, Queen of Australia. This title was introduced in 1973. The Queen is represented in Australia by the Governor-General who is appointed on the recommendation of the Prime Minister of Australia. The Governor-General has been delegated virtually all powers that The Queen holds as the formal Australian Head of State.

Based on the colonial arrangements before Federation in 1901, each State has a Governor who represents The Queen. The Governor is appointed on the recommendation of the Premier of the State. The appointment of the Administrator in the Northern Territory is slightly different as the appointment is made by the Governor-General on the recommendation of the Chief Minister with the agreement of the Prime Minister. The Governors have been delegated virtually all the powers enjoyed by the Governor-General as far as State matters are concerned. There are some matters which have a national implication which Governors refer to the Governor-General, either for decision or as a matter of courtesy. Other than in these cases, the representation is a direct one and reporting through the Governor-General is not required.

The Royal Family

Visits to Australia by The Queen and other members of the Royal Family were quite frequent during the 1970s and 1980s. The Queen visited almost every second year and other family members, particularly the Prince of Wales, visited regularly. This pattern changed during the 1990s with very few visits taking place. The Queen made a major visit during the bicentennial year of 1988, made a short visit to New South Wales in 1990 and then did not visit again until 2000. The Queen makes these visits on the invitation of the Governor-General, who acts on the advice of the Australian Prime Minister.

There have been visits by members of the Royal Family during the 1990s but these have been private where the invitation has come from an organisation or a State government. There was some publicity for the visit by the Princess Royal (Princess Anne) during the Olympic Games where she undertook engagements associated with the Olympics as well as some relating to her position as president of the Save the Children's Fund. These visits are not regarded as official.

Even with the unofficial visits, there is a very thorough preparation programme. A member of the visitor's staff, normally accompanied by a police protection officer, will visit Australia to develop and agree to the programme with the Australian hosts some months before the visit. Sometimes, there are two visits. The programme is developed in minute detail. The location and number of media representatives, the mixture of still photographers, television crews and journalists, their entry and exit and the security arrangements for the media pool, are all determined exactly for each venue.

The great strength of this very detailed preparation is that once the programme has been agreed to, it is never altered at the last minute. This should not be taken to indicate a lack of flexibility. Of course, there are changes made to fit the circumstances on the day, but they are the obvious and sensible ones, not major variations to the basic programme. Although the preparatory period can be tiresome in the attention to detail required, the programme delivery on the day is very easy. This cannot be said for most other visitors at the Head of State or Head of Government level.

I don't intend to set out any specific guidelines on what you should do if you are included as a venue for a Royal visitor. There will be plenty of advice from skilled Commonwealth and State protocol officers during the preparatory period.

Some of the recurring questions that are asked (with a few answers) are:

- Should I curtsy or bow? Although it has been traditional for ladies to curtsy and gentlemen to bow on presentation to a member of the Royal Family, this is not expected or required. You only have to watch television pictures of The Queen attending quite formal occasions in the United Kingdom to see that this does not always happen there now. It is a matter of personal choice. However, if you feel you would like to do so, ladies should remember that you have to come up as far as you go down - a short 'bob' is probably the safest option. For men, it is a head bow - just a nod of the head. It should not be a bow from the waist.

- Should I wear a hat and gloves? Although The Queen invariably wears a hat and gloves, there is no requirement for others to do so. If you normally wear a hat and gloves and feel comfortable doing so, and it is appropriate for the occasion, then by all means wear them. There would not be too many people in Australia to whom this guideline would apply! The last thing you want to do is to pull the 'duty hat' from the back of the wardrobe, which was last worn in 1992 to a cousin's wedding, jam it on your head and feel uncomfortable all day. (You didn't even like the hat at the wedding).
- What should I wear? My mother told me that I should not wear a black dress. Although some may use the excuse of attending a Royal function as a reason for getting a new outfit, there is no need to do so. Wear an outfit that you like and feel comfortable wearing. This particularly applies to shoes. There is always a lot of standing around, arriving early, and so on associated with Royal functions and the last thing you need to be wearing is a pair of very fashionable but highly uncomfortable new shoes. The black dress is an old wives' tale. Where would most females be without their 'little black number'?
- How do I address The Queen (or other member of the Royal Family)? There are some detailed rules on this but, as with the curtsy and the bow, it is a matter of choice. The safest form of greeting to The Queen is "Your Majesty" or "Ma'am". Note that "Ma'am" is pronounced to rhyme with 'Pam'. It is **not** pronounced as you hear so often on television period dramas as "Marm". With other female members of the Royal Family use "Your Royal Highness" or "Ma'am". With male members the address is "Your Royal Highness" or "Sir". You will find that meetings are very relaxed and you will be into the conversation while you are still trying to think what you should say as a greeting. Provided the greeting is courteous, the actual words are not really important.

- Can I present The Queen with a small gift? It is unlikely that a gift will be accepted as there are, unfortunately, security considerations. Anyone seen carrying a wrapped item, however small, is likely to find themselves the attention of a security officer. The Queen does accept small posies of flowers, preferably from children when on 'walkabouts'. The posy should be tied with ribbon or secured with plastic clips. Avoid wire or other metallic fastenings. This is the best way to go but make sure there is a card firmly attached with your name and address so that you can subsequently receive a note of appreciation from the Lady-in-Waiting accompanying The Queen.
- How do I write to The Queen? Unless you are personally known to The Queen (in which case you don't want this advice), it is best to write to the private secretary and request him to advise The Queen on the subject of your letter. It should be addressed to:

The Private Secretary to The Queen
Buckingham Palace
LONDON SW1 1AA
UNITED KINGDOM

The salutation in the letter is "Dear Sir" and the conclusion is "Yours sincerely".

Vice-Regal Representation

The Vice-Regal representatives in Australia are the Governor-General, the Governors of the States and the Administrator of the Northern Territory. They carry out the constitutional duties of a Head of State as The Queen's representative in their respective jurisdictions but are most frequently seen and met by Australians at community or social functions. They travel widely and are frequent visitors to communities and community activities.

There has been a subtle change in recent years which has expanded the role of some Governors beyond being solely the representative of The Queen within their jurisdictions. In some States, the Premiers have asked the Governor to travel overseas to represent the State (rather than The Queen) on missions relating to sister-state relationships and also to encourage trade and cultural links. Such assignments have been most successful. To purists this is moving beyond the constitutional duties of the Governors, but it does demonstrate the changes that occur over time.

A visit by the Governor-General or a Governor does not require the detailed preparation associated with a Royal visit that has previously been described, but you will still have to ensure your preparations are thorough. There may be a prior visit by a member of staff and possibly a visit from the appropriate police service. At the very least there will be a number of telephone conversations and the requirement to provide a detailed order of arrangements. This should clearly set out what the Governor-General or Governor is being requested to do and who will be responsible for escorting. Details of the seating arrangements at any meals will also be required.

Some commonly asked questions are:

- Should I curtsy or bow? It was traditional practice for Vice-Regal representatives (and the spouse of the Governor-General) to be accorded the same courtesies as The Queen in this regard. This is now not generally followed. If there is no expectation by The Queen that people should curtsy or bow, there is **absolutely** no expectation on the part of the Vice-Regal representatives. It is now very rarely seen and then generally only from senior citizens who were raised in more traditional times.

- How do I address the Governor-General or Governor? The formal method of address is "Your Excellency" or "Sir/Ma'am" with "Ma'am" being pronounced as previously described. As mentioned elsewhere, the spouse of the Governor-General is similarly addressed but this does not apply to spouses of Governors. The Administrator of the Northern Territory is addressed as "Your Honour" or "Sir/Ma'am". Some Vice-Regal representatives feel that being addressed as "Your Excellency" is too formal for Australia in the 21st century and prefer to be addressed as "Governor". Ask this question of a member of the staff during the reconnaissance meetings to establish the preferred form and follow that.

- Should we fly a flag or play the National Anthem during the Governor-General's/Governor's visit? Each Vice-Regal representative has a distinctive personal flag. It is flown on respective Government Houses and a small version in the form of a car pennant is normally flown on the Vice-Regal car. The full-sized personal flag may be flown at other venues during a visit but there is no compulsion to do so. It is only flown while the Governor-General or Governor is present. The matter of anthems and the Vice-Regal salute are covered elsewhere. It is best to discuss these matters with the staff during the reconnaissance phase. They can normally arrange to provide a flag and a tape or CD of the appropriate music. What is important is that the use of the flag or the anthem appears natural and sensible. It should add to the occasion. It must not appear contrived.

For Further Information

- Contact the appropriate protocol office listed in Appendix A.
- Contact the Governor-General's website at *www.gg.gov.au* This site has links to all Governor's web sites.
- Contact the British Monarchy website at *www.royal.gov.uk* for general information on the Royal Family.

* * *

The Prince and Princess of Wales visited Sovereign Hill Historical Park in Ballarat. Before the lunch there was a five-minute comfort stop in the United States Hotel and the front bar of the hotel was reserved for the official party. It was a bitterly cold Ballarat day and, on entering, the barman welcomed everyone in colonial style and asked what they would like to drink. Without hesitation, Prince Charles asked for a double scotch and everyone was happy to follow the leader. As he stood at one end of the polished wood bar, Charles commented that this looked like one of those bars you see in cowboy movies where tankards of beer are slid from one end to the other. The alert barman immediately produced a large glass tankard filled with beer which Charles then despatched along the length of the bar. The Prince's Scotland Yard security officer was standing at the far end of the bar and had not been watching what was happening. Charles called to him, "Colin, here's your beer." Being a good police officer, he had not had a warming scotch and was probably still partially frozen. Whatever, his reactions weren't fast enough. The tankard hit the far wall and smashed to pieces. We left the bar for lunch shortly thereafter.

GIFTS

Australia is not a major gift-giving nation. Gifts are given to friends at birthdays and at some major festivals such as Christmas but there is no ritual of gift exchanging related to business such as exists in Japan.

There is generally no great concern on whether to give gifts and what form that gift should take when dealing with visitors from Western countries who share similar democratic, racial and religious backgrounds to our own. There is generally more concern when dealing with visitors from countries with which we are not so familiar and where customs, beliefs, and possibly superstitions, are not so well known to us.

In the past 20 years there has been an explosion of information throughout the world caused by the advance of television, the internet, improved communication systems and greatly increased world travel. Societies which tended to be closed or restrictive are now much more open and the official or business traveller is now much more aware of Western society and the Western way of life. Errors in gift-giving that may have caused offence and concern in the past are now not so important. The foreign recipient is much more understanding.

However, that is not to say that we should not think carefully about what gifts should be given. A gift which is really appreciated and which does not violate any guidelines is always much better than one pulled from the standard gift cupboard at the last minute.

Here are a few general comments on gifts:

- It is useful to draw a distinction between gifts and mementoes. A gift is a carefully selected article which you hope will be appreciated and used or displayed by the recipient. A memento is a reminder of the visit or meeting. A memento may or may not survive the hotel rubbish bin. In general terms, a gift will be more expensive than a memento. Mementoes frequently have the company name or logo displayed whereas a gift will have a much more subtle reminder of the donor. Examples of mementoes would include ball point pens, business card holders, ties, sleeve links and pocket diaries.
- Gifts should always be wrapped.
- Most international visitors travel in the same type of commercial aircraft as you do. The last thing they need is a fragile, bulky or heavy gift which they will have to try to fit into their luggage. Small, light items generally make the most acceptable gifts.
- Gifts need not be expensive.

- Australian craft items are a good choice. These can vary from semi-novelty items worth only a few dollars to exquisite silver and gold items worth considerably more.
- With government officials, some countries have restrictions on the value of gifts that officers can receive. The Australian Government has a financial limitation on the value of gifts that their Ministers may keep. Any gift above the established value must be surrendered and becomes government property.
- Avoid personal gifts such as specialised jewellery and perfume.
- Make sure a gift or memento is not manufactured in the country of the recipient (or cannot be identified as such!)
- If giving a book to a non-English speaking visitor, go for a pictorial, coffee-table-style publication with a minimum of text.
- Keep a record of what gifts and mementoes are given to whom and which organisation they represent. There is nothing worse than making the same presentation in a year's time.
- The source of a gift should be subtly shown. It may be a small plaque attached underneath or on the rear of the item. In the case of a box, it may be attached inside the lid. In the case of a framed picture, the name of the picture and presentation details should be shown on the rear, not the front of the painting.
- A signed presentation card or short personal note may be included with the gift (but inside the wrapping).

It is not intended to give a list of 'do's and don'ts' of gift-giving for every country but some general guidelines on matters that should be considered for visitors from countries near Australia may be a help.

- <u>Japan</u>

    The exchange of gifts and mementoes is traditional.

Avoid items which are clearly made of plastic. This is hard to do today but, for example, metal cuff links are preferable to plastic ones.

The wrapping of the gift is almost as important as the gift itself. If a gift is irregular in shape, place it in a box so that the presented package is very neat and tidy. Don't use black and white paper. (Don't get David Jones to wrap the gifts!)

Avoid giving a set of four of anything.

Gifts are normally not opened at the time of receipt.

- People's Republic of China

    Chinese always seem to travel in groups. Give one gift to the leader of the delegation on behalf of all members. You may consider a memento for all members of the party but they should all receive the same (including the leader).

    Give gifts with both hands. Gifts are not normally opened at the time of receipt.

    Gifts should not appear to be excessively expensive. If so, this could cause problems on return to China.

    Avoid white, black or blue wrapping. Red is a lucky colour and is a good wrapping paper choice.

    Even numbers are better than odd numbers: eight is a particularly lucky number.

- Indonesia

    The exchange of small gifts is traditional.

    With Muslim Indonesians avoid pork, alcohol and pig-skin products.

    Gifts are not normally opened at the time of receipt.

- Malaysia

    With Muslim Malays avoid pork, alcohol and pig-skin products.

    Gifts are not normally opened at the time of receipt.

    Avoid white wrapping paper which is a colour associated with death, especially for Chinese Malays.

- Thailand

    Avoid gifts made of wood. Wood is considered a low-grade commodity.

    Gifts are not normally opened at the time of receipt.

For Further Information

- Contact the appropriate protocol office listed in Appendix A.
- The book *Kiss, Bow or Shake Hands* also has some useful information on gift-giving to foreign visitors.

* * *

The Governor was having the Japanese Ambassador and his wife stay at Government House for the weekend as private guests. Both parties had been invited to a performance of the Australian Ballet on the Saturday night and the Governor, who had hit it off very successfully with the Ambassador during an earlier official visit, had invited them to stay.

On the Saturday morning, a newly appointed aide was dispatched to the airport to meet the Ambassador and his wife and escort them to Government House. On the appointed flight from Canberra, a very well-dressed Japanese couple were the first off the aircraft, were greeted by the aide and, after collecting the luggage, were driven to Government House. Both spoke excellent English and were very interested in all they were being shown and told.

On arrival at Government House, the Governor found himself greeting a Japanese couple he had never seen before in his life. A professor from a Japanese university, the keynote speaker at a medical conference, was equally amazed at the ambience of his lodgings and the efficiency of his airport transfer.

The matter was sorted out over a cup of tea. The Japanese Ambassador and his wife arrived by taxi about 40 minutes later.

There is a message here for someone.

Chapter 2

Hospitality

HOSPITALITY FUNCTIONS

This section will deal with official or corporate hospitality rather than private hospitality at home. It is aimed at the more formal type of function but should still be useful in making arrangements for something more casual. It will not tell you how to set a table or what coloured napkins should be used for a particular type of function. There is plenty of that type of advice in social etiquette books, which are readily available. What will be discussed is the planning and logistics necessary to arrange a successful official function whether it be a luncheon, dinner or cocktail reception.

The trend in Australia in recent years has been towards more informal arrangements in almost everything we do. This also applies to hospitality functions. However, the amount of work and preparation necessary for a successful, less formal function is only marginally below that required for a state banquet.

The guidelines suggested should not be regarded as the 'only way', the 'necessary way' or the 'best way'. Every function is different. With good planning and an approach of 'courtesy and consideration', the function is well on the way to being a success.

Official functions are usually held to:

- Welcome an important dignitary or visiting group.
- To thank an individual or group for their contribution to your organisation.
- To launch a new initiative.
- To mark a milestone or anniversary.

The essential steps are:

- Decide on the format of the function, including the budget, and select an appropriate venue.
- Prepare a draft running sheet.
- Prepare your guest list and issue invitations.
- Meet the venue manager and the caterer to discuss menu and format.
- Develop administrative details such as deciding seating arrangements and then printing menus, name/place cards and seating plans.

Format of the Function

The purpose of the function, or perhaps the availability of the guest of honour, will usually determine the form the function should take.

- The dinner is probably the most formal but usually allows for a more relaxed atmosphere as there is no pressure to get away for that next business meeting which so often exists with a luncheon. A good attendance by spouses is more likely. There is also an expectation of something more in the form of entertainment and more formal surroundings.

- The luncheon is generally aimed at business activities and spouses/partners are often unable to attend. There is always a degree of time pressure with luncheons, with some guests arriving late or having to depart before the luncheon programme is finished.
- The cocktail reception (or drinks/nibbles associated with an announcement or launch) is ideal where there are a number of people to be met and it is important that guests have a chance to speak to many of the other guests. It is the least formal of all forms of hospitality and allows a large degree of flexibility for late arrivals and early departures should this be necessary. Receptions also allow greater flexibility on numbers who can be invited and this ensures a few 'no-shows' do not spoil the function. Cocktail receptions are not as highly regarded as luncheons or dinners.

Budget

The budget can get away from you if you do not consider all the possible expenses. The following possible costs should be considered:

- Food and beverage, including additional serving staff costs.
- Venue hire, including any special cleaning costs or surcharge for additional time.
- Hire of tables, chairs, linen, cutlery.
- Flowers or other decorations
- Sound system, dais, lectern
- Entertainment
- Small gifts or mementoes
- Additional security staff

- Printing of invitations, place cards etc, postage
- Administrative costs of staff during the preparatory and conduct stages

Venue

Venues can vary from an established in-house entertainment area to a 'bare' facility where you have to hire the caterer separately and arrange many of the decoration aspects yourself, through to a hotel or reception venue where the catering and most of the support facilities will come as a packaged deal. The latter are obviously administratively more simple and are not necessarily more expensive. However, with hotels you will be using a venue that anyone else can use and it will not be special for your function. "Oh, no," you can hear some guests saying, "not another dinner at the Grand!" An unusual venue raises the anticipation of the guests and this can play a major part in getting the function off to a good start. However, it is not very practical to arrange a luncheon at an unusual venue that is 30 minutes' drive out of the city when most of your guests are working in the city during the day.

The following matters should be considered:

- Is the size right and does it have space, in the case of a luncheon or dinner, for the assembly of guests for drinks before moving into the dining room?
- Does the ambience of the venue suit the type of function you want to deliver? Can it be changed?
- Is there a separate room for the official party if you wished to structure the function that way?
- Is parking readily available?
- Does it have facilities for the disabled in terms of access and rest-room facilities?

- Is it suitable for news media coverage of the event if this is important to the function?

The relationship you establish with the service providers, whether they be an individual caterer, a hotel or a function venue coordinator, is very important. Cooperation will be based on a regular and professional two-way exchange of information which will lead to a feeling of confidence on both sides. It is important that you ask the advice of the chef in compiling your menu. You may have a particular dish in mind, but if the chef is not confident of being able to deliver a top-class product, some compromise may be prudent. Your desire may have to be varied on the availability of suitable fresh produce or professional advice on how your selection would present on the plate.

Bear in mind that yours will only be one of many functions being held at a particular hotel or function venue and they will not start to focus on yours until a few days before the event. To keep venue operators 'on the boil', it is a good idea to contact them about once a week to show them you are serious. Don't telephone them and say, "How are things going?" Have a couple of specific questions to ask which require them to think and give a positive response. However, keep the amount of general contact in perspective. Too little and you may be neglected; too much and you may be regarded as a pest.

Format

An established format to which all participants agree is vital. This is normally expected for a formal function, but it is equally important for less formal ones. If you don't plan the informality, there is a real danger that the function will run away from you and will become less enjoyable than you planned.

A format that is growing in favour at both luncheons and dinners is to have all the formalities before the meal is served. This is frequently known as the 'Chinese format' as all their banquets are conducted this way. It has the following advantages:

- The speakers and the audience are fresh and alert.
- The content of the speeches can be used as the basis for initial conversation at the tables, especially where the guests are not well known to one another.
- The host and the guest of honour can relax during the meal, having 'sung for their supper'.
- In business situations, guests who may have to leave the meal early for other appointments do not miss the speeches.
- The caterers can operate with confidence knowing that there is less chance of a dish being spoiled due to speeches of unpredictable length occurring mid-meal.

If this format is followed, the time for speeches must not exceed 30 minutes, with 15-20 minutes being preferable. Apart from bread/bread rolls, there should be no food placed on the tables. Watching a smoked salmon entree slowly curling at the edges is not very appetising! However, there should be a glass of water and a glass of wine already poured.

Speeches

Who is going to speak is a vital element. Everyone enjoys and expects a speech or two, but the enthusiasm wanes when there are three or four or more. There is a finite amount of information which can make up a relevant and interesting address and to hear the same thing said by a variety of people, many of whom are not orators, becomes boring. We have all been to functions where guests towards the rear of the room start talking among themselves during a speech. It is not always the fault of the individual speaker - perhaps there have just been too many speeches.

The ideal is probably two: the host to welcome and the guest of honour to deliver the message. Frequently, a third speaker is introduced to thank the guest speaker, but you need to consider whether this is really necessary. If you decide to go ahead with that arrangement, ensure that the thank-you comments are short. There have been occasions where the person delivering the thanks has spoken for as long as the guest of honour!

However, there will be occasions where there is pressure for a variety of speakers. This is especially so in government circles where every Minister or Mayor who has been involved in a project or whose organisation has provided some funding wants to speak. It is noticeable how this desire increases a few months out from an election or if television cameras are present!

If possible, try to offer each speaker some particular aspect that can form the centrepiece of their address. This gives some focus and helps ensure that the same speech is not given three times. This procedure is particularly welcomed by the later speakers who run the risk of having all their thunder stolen by those who spoke before them.

It is best to have all the speeches together. Having a segment of speaking after each course can spoil the event by leaving the impression that the function has been dominated by speeches (which is often the case).

The Running Sheet

A draft running sheet should be prepared very early in the planning. It will be modified frequently as arrangements progress and it should be seen as a flexible document, especially in the early stages. Initially, it should show every step that is to be taken but the final running sheet may omit some of the basic administrative detail. Bear in mind that everything takes longer than you initially plan. You have to wait for those last couple of guests who are running late or the guest speaker, who agreed to speak for 15 minutes, somehow delivers a 25-minute address on the day. Caterers, no matter how good or experienced they are, invariably take longer to serve the meal than originally promised. There is always some 'crisis' in the kitchen.

An example of an early running sheet could be:

**RUNNING SHEET
FOR DINNER IN HONOUR OF THE VISIT BY
THE HONOURABLE ROBERT BICKETT MP
MINISTER FOR PRODUCTION
AND MRS DIANE BICKETT
THURSDAY 26 NOVEMBER**

1730	Angela Smith, Alexandra Karadaglis, Peter Matheson and Rebecca Sullivan arrive at the Mountain View Reception Centre. Meet function coordinator Rania Wehbi (0486 853 188) and confirm arrangements. Layout seating cards on the table in the foyer, layout place cards and menus on the tables, check cleanliness of rest rooms, test public address system, check floral decorations are in place (Greenway Florists - 0486 237 984).
1800	The string quartet, Red Alert, arrives. (Leader Rob Jefferson - 0486 224 976)
1815	The photographer arrives. (Katie White - 0486 976 443)
1820	Check lights in the carpark and walkway to the entrance are switched on.
1830	The host, Mr Brendan Bannan and Mrs Jenny Bannan arrive (0486 353 778). Walk through the arrangements with them including the seating at the official table.
1840	Band in position in the pre-drinks area. Cloak room staffed. Mr and Mrs Bannan at the entrance to greet guests. Drink waiting staff on duty in the pre-drinks area. Seating card desk staffed.

1845	Guests commence arriving. Receive seating cards and welcomed at the entrance to the pre-drinks area by:
	
	    Mr Brendan Bannan
	    General Manager, Idaho Corporation
	    and Mrs Jenny Bannan
	
	Band commences playing and refreshments are served.

1900	The Honourable Robert Bickett, Minister for Production and Mrs Bickett arrive at the entrance and are met by Peter Matheson, Public Affairs Manager, and escorted to the pre-drinks area where they are greeted by the host.

1910	Advise Mr Bannan that all guests have arrived and the move to the dining room can commence.
	Pre-pouring of wine and chilled water on all tables commences.
	Steward on duty at the entrance to the dining room to collect guests' glasses.
	The doors to the dining room are opened. Angela Smith and Alexandra Karadaglis move through the pre-drinks area personally inviting guests to move to their places for dinner. Peter Matheson at the entrance to the dining room with a seating plan to assist any guests who have mislaid their seating cards.
1920	Guests are seated. The Master of Ceremonies, Andrew Campbell, briefly welcomes the guests and introduces:
	Mr Brendan Bannan *General Manager, Idaho Corporation*
	Mr Bannan speaks and concludes with a toast to the success of the Unterlaken Project.
1935	Andrew Campbell introduces:
	The Honourable Bob Bickett MP *Minister for Productivity*
	The Minister speaks.
1945	The entree course is served.
	Etc Etc Etc

Guest Lists and Invitations

These matters are discussed fully in a separate section.

Entertainment

Entertainment can play a major part in the success of a function but it needs to be carefully chosen. Do you want to have background music played throughout the function or are you going to have a specific entertainment segment or segments as part of the programme?

The background music requirement can be met by playing suitable music over the public address system. You choose the music, you decide the volume and you decide when it is played and when it is not. It is also cheap. What you lose is the ambience of a musical group performing and recorded music can sound like muzak in a supermarket. However, a string quartet at one end of a room is probably not heard or seen by most of the guests. If they play at a volume to be heard by all, those near the group will have an uncomfortable evening. If you place them on a dais so that they can be seen, they tend to become 'an act' and may expect to be listened to as an entertainment rather than just providing background music. Groups with such an expectation tend to play louder to get attention, especially if they are larger than a quintet. String groups are usually safe, but once wind instruments are introduced, the volume level invariably increases. Live background music can be great but the choice of the group requires careful attention. They should specialise in providing background music and clearly understand that they are not the star turn of the night.

The choice of a stand-alone entertainment act can also add to the occasion. The choice needs to match the event. The style of entertainment for a football break-up night will differ considerably from the managing director's annual dinner. It is wise to have seen the act before rather than just accepting a written description from a brochure or taking the word of a talent agent whose livelihood relies on selling it.

The quantity of entertainment is often overdone with too many segments or one segment lasting too long. The guests towards the back of the room lose interest and start to talk among themselves. The cost of live entertainment can be surprisingly high and if the singer will provide eight songs for the basic engagement price, there is a great temptation to 'get your money's worth'. In reality, the programme would be better balanced with 15 minutes of entertainment, say five songs, rather than 25 minutes for all eight items. It takes a strong planner to put quality ahead of quantity in such cases.

Seating

The table layout should be decided by the host to fit the style of the function in consultation with the caterer. Some frequently used formats are:

- Round or rectangular tables
- A single rectangular table
- U- or T-shaped tables
- A long official table (now rarely used)

The once-familiar formal arrangement of a long table with seating on one side only with the official guests facing the other guests who are seated at round or rectangular tables is now rarely used. Even at very formal functions, all guests are now usually seated at round tables. This arrangement has the advantage of allowing all guests to converse more readily and also allows a more convivial atmosphere to develop.

The general principle of official seating is that the guest of honour is placed on the host's right and the guest of honour's spouse is placed on the host's left. The host's spouse is then placed on the right of the guest of honour. If spouses are not present, the second most important guest is placed on the host's left. Other guests are normally allocated to tables in their order of importance to the host organisation. Some examples are shown below.

WHO'S WHO GUIDE TO PROTOCOL

LUNCHEON OR DINNER - ROUND TABLES

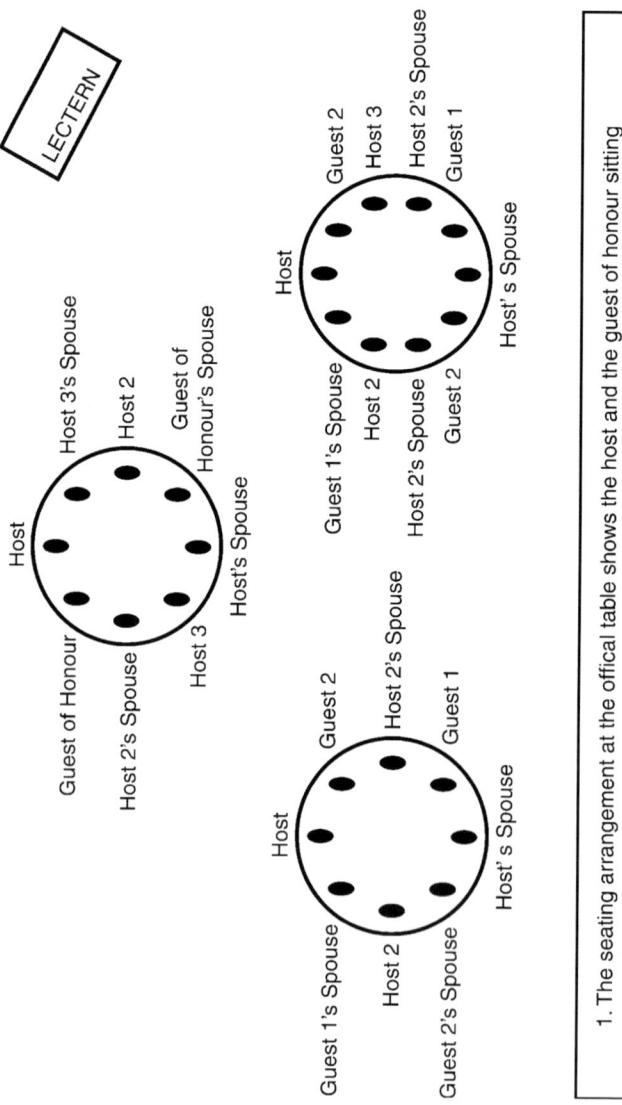

LECTERN

Table 1 (8 seats):
- Host
- Host 2
- Host 3's Spouse
- Host 2
- Guest of Honour's Spouse
- Host's Spouse
- Host 3
- Host 2's Spouse
- Guest of Honour

Table 2 (10 seats):
- Host
- Guest 2
- Guest 3
- Host 2's Spouse
- Guest 1
- Host's Spouse
- Guest 2
- Host 2's Spouse
- Host 2
- Guest 1's Spouse

Table 3 (8 seats):
- Host
- Guest 2
- Host 2's Spouse
- Guest 1
- Host's Spouse
- Guest 2's Spouse
- Host 2
- Guest 1's Spouse

1. The seating arrangement at the offical table shows the host and the guest of honour sitting together and the respective spouses sitting together. With a setting of 8, alternate male/female seating is possible for other guests but this is not so for a table of 10.
2. Other tables show an alternate seating arrangement with two guest at each table. 10 settings are necessary to achieve alternate male/female and guest/host.
3. The lectern should be close to the offical table.
4. It would be unusual for the offical table to be raised in these circumstances.

34

Hospitality

SINGLE RECTANGULAR TABLE SEATING

U, T AND HOLLOW SQUARE SEATING

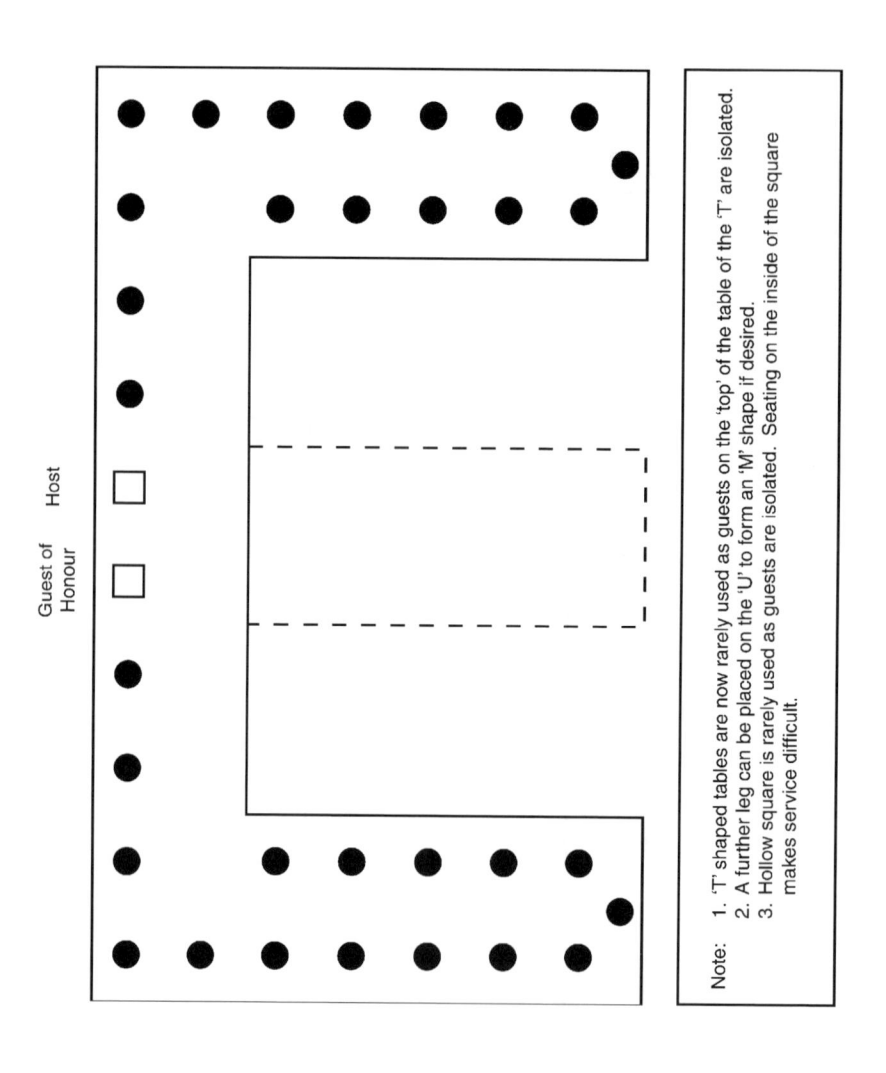

Guest of Honour — Host

Note:
1. 'T' shaped tables are now rarely used as guests on the 'top' of the table of the 'T' are isolated.
2. A further leg can be placed on the 'U' to form an 'M' shape if desired.
3. Hollow square is rarely used as guests are isolated. Seating on the inside of the square makes service difficult.

THE LONG OFFICIAL TABLE SEATING

LECTERN

- Host 3's Spouse
- Guest 2's Spouse
- Host 2
- Guest of Honour's Spouse
- Host
- Guest of Honour
- Host's Spouse
- Guest 2
- Host 2's Spouse
- Host 3

Private Secretary

ADC

The following general guidelines may be helpful:

- Important members of the inviting body (deputy hosts) should be interspersed among the principal guests.
- Couples should always be seated at the same table but it is up to the host to decide whether partners are seated together or next to other guests. The latter procedure is the normal arrangement as it gives everyone an opportunity to meet new faces. If one of the partners does not speak English, they should be seated together for practical reasons.
- At business functions less emphasis may be placed on precedence when arranging seating. It may be better for people to be placed next to those with whom they can most usefully talk.
- Males and females should be seated alternately.
- At a predominantly male function, when not all guests are accompanied by their wives or partners, it is best to seat two female partners at the same table rather than having them seated at separate tables.
- If a long official table is used, try to avoid having a female sitting at the end of the table.
- Speeches may be made from the table, but it is preferable to have them delivered from a separate lectern set to one side of the table. This has the advantage of:
    - not disturbing the table settings and decorations by a table lectern and microphone;
    - the table lectern and microphone do not have to be moved along or around the table for other speakers; and
    - adequate lighting can be provided onto the lectern should this be needed for photographic or television coverage. This avoids difficult spotlighting of the official table.
- The official table is sometimes raised on a dais but this is becoming less common, especially with the use of round tables.

Any elevation should not be too high - 25 cm would normally be sufficient - but even in a large hall the height should not exceed 50 cm.

- If the long official table format is used on a dais, the front of the table must be enclosed.
- Table numbers must be of a good size and elevated above the level of the menus and any table decorations. It is useful to number the tables from the point of entry into the dining room rather than numbering the official table as Table 1 and then running back and forth across the room. There is nothing more frustrating than following a line of numbers to one side of the room expecting to find your table, only to find that you are in the next row at the other end of the room. It is usually best to name the official table as such and not give it a number.
- In the case of Vice-Regal guests, the accompanying staff (for example, aide, personal assistant or secretary) should not be seated at the official table. They should be seated at an adjacent table and in a position where eye contact between the principal and the staff member is possible.
- If the guest of honour is accompanied by a police security team, they will normally ask to be seated at a table near the entrances to the room. They will always conduct a prior reconnaissance. If you know that security officers will be present, ascertain their seating requirements before finalising the seating plan. They should not be identified as security officers on any printed plan. Use personal names or a phrase such as 'Prime Minister's Staff'.
- On occasions, interpreters will be required. In some countries, interpreters sit behind the important guests and do not eat. Australia tends to adopt a more egalitarian approach. Interpreters are normally seated at the table and are served a meal with the other guests (they still often do not get much of a chance to eat it!). In the case of the host and the guest of honour, the

interpreter should not sit between them. It is normal for the interpreter to sit on the right side of the guest of honour. If there are speeches, a separate microphone, normally placed on a stand to the side of the lectern, will be required for the interpreter.

News Media Representatives

News media representatives will be present at some functions and positive arrangements should be made. They are usually present to record the speeches. At luncheons and dinners there are some advantages in adopting the procedure of having the speeches before the meal. The news media can cover that part of the proceedings with some certainty regarding time and then leave to file their stories. It is always appreciated if a separate room can be set aside with some light refreshments, which can be used by the journalists while waiting for the speeches to begin.

Arrangements should be made for photographers and television crews to have good access to the speeches without obstructing the view of other guests. A media riser, which will allow them to photograph over the heads of other guests, may be needed. Radio journalists and television sound technicians appreciate a splitter box to ensure they get good quality sound - otherwise you may end up with several microphones taped to the microphone on the lectern which can interfere with the general sound quality. Some VIPs object to speaking into a 'forest' of microphones.

Some media representatives may ask to interview the guest of honour or other guests either before, or immediately after, the function. Many VIPs will not agree to being 'ambushed' whereas others may be quite amenable to a doorstop interview. If you know this may happen, it is best to check with the guest of honour's staff before the function. If the request comes from the media on the day, it is frequently best to refuse such requests on the territory you control and suggest that any impromptu interviews be conducted in the hotel lobby or on the street outside the venue. In the case of politicians, the topics of the interview frequently have nothing to do with the function that has just been attended.

Separate Official Party Room

When you wish to have the official party enter the dining room in a ceremonial manner after all the other guests are seated, it is almost essential to have a separate room in which the official party can gather to have their pre-function drinks. This arrangement is also useful where there are a number of important guests who cannot be seated at the official table but you wish to do something special for them. Even if this is not the case, it is useful to have more than just the official table guests in the separate room. Eight or 10 people who will be sitting together for the meal will appreciate having other people to speak to before the meal.

The time in a separate room should not be great and those who are invited may be asked to arrive after the other guests. The time in the room should not exceed 20 minutes. Bear in mind that it will take a minimum of 10 minutes for the general guests to be seated, so if you invited the official party to arrive about 10-15 minutes before you intend to begin seating, that would be about right.

The other official party room guests who are not seated at the official table should be asked to move to their tables just a minute or so before the ceremonial entry begins. Make sure you have told them of these arrangements beforehand.

The Meal

Again, quality is more important than quantity. Everyone seems to be on a diet of some description these days and meals consisting of five courses are not particularly welcome. Generally, a dinner will consist of three courses followed by coffee and possibly petit fours. Luncheons are generally two-course affairs with an entree and a main course followed by coffee. A cheese and greens platter for the table may accompany the coffee. A few comments on the choice of meals:

- The host should choose the menu for all guests. The practice of having alternate main courses (steak for the men, chicken for the ladies!) is really passé.
- Avoid meals that are smothered in sauces. It is best if the caterer can place any accompanying sauce on the side of the plate.
- Avoid items that may be difficult for some guests, such as pork.
- All courses should have the appearance of fresh and healthy food. Avoid deep-fried or oily foods. Fresh berries with separate pouring cream is usually a better choice for dessert than cheese cake or a rich pudding.
- Ensure the caterer has a vegetarian option available for both the entree and the main course.
- The main course should always be a hot meal but cold entrees and desserts are quite acceptable.
- Silver service of the main course was once regarded as the ultimate in food presentation and service. As this skill among waiting staff has declined to a point of almost non-existence, silver service should be avoided. The meal is frequently cold and invariably not very attractively presented. Plated service from the kitchen is the way to go.
- Avoid serving what we may regard as a 'national meal' to visiting foreign dignitaries. Despite all claims by the chef (even if he is

a national of the country concerned), the meal will never match the home standard. Serve good Western dishes that we understand.

- Buffet meals are often considered to be faster than table service. This is a misnomer as anyone who has stood in a queue behind someone who takes two minutes to make their selection will know. If you do decide to have a buffet meal, you should allow one buffet table for every 20-25 guests if you do not want the meal to take a very long time.

With a cocktail reception there should be a mixture of both hot and cold canapés. It is important that they should be bite-sized as far as possible. A few points to consider:

- Sandwiches should not be overfilled. Triangle sandwiches should have the crusts removed. Ribbon sandwiches are often preferable.
- Food with a fresh and healthy appearance is better than greasy, deep-fried items. Some popular cocktail items have to be fried but ensure that they comprise no more than 30% of the menu selections.
- Avoid serving items where guests are left holding the bones - for example, chicken pieces, unless there are sufficient small dishes placed around the room.
- Variety of appearance and texture, including at least one vegetarian item, is important.
- Avoid items that are likely to 'leak' from the bottom leaving a trail of grease or sauce down the guest's dress or tie. With items that may do this (some of the popular cocktail food items), ensure they are small enough to be eaten in one bite.
- Small paper napkins should be available with all food offered.
- It is best to have only one selection of food on a platter. There is nothing worse than being offered a platter with three of the

four choices already taken - you know you are being offered the least popular item. With one item per platter the guest has only one choice - take it or leave it!

- Ensure that the waiting staff stop serving when three quarters of the platter has been used. They should return to the kitchen to replenish and freshen up the appearance of the serving tray (including the replacement of any soiled doilies or tired decoration).

- All service, both food and beverage, should cease during the speeches.

The Beverages

At cocktail receptions and for pre-luncheon and pre-dinner drinks, the first choice is whether to have a restricted selection of beverages or whether there will be an open bar.

The restricted bar is more common at luncheon functions where time is frequently short and there is probably a preference by the guests for a refreshing rather than an alcoholic drink. There is generally not much of a call for a double scotch in the middle of the day - if there is, keep an eye on that guest! A restricted bar would normally consist of a still white wine, a red wine, beer (both full-strength and light), orange juice and mineral water. Sparkling Australian wine in the style of champagne is also often included and there are many high-quality, reasonably priced varieties available. These items should be presented by waiting staff with a full selection on each tray. It is not practicable for waiting staff to take and fulfil individual orders - the majority of guests will never see a drink.

A full bar is normal at cocktail receptions and for pre-dinner drinks. The range of drinks is not restricted, although complicated fancy cocktails would not normally be offered. However, it is important to have a well-trained barman who can mix a good martini (either

Hospitality

shaken or stirred) should that be requested. The selection of drinks offered would include those for a restricted bar plus some spirits, principally scotch and gin. Orders would be taken for those who requested slightly less popular mixed drinks based on rum or brandy. Other drinks would only be included on the tray if you knew of a particular preference by this group of guests.

Some hotels and reception venues offer a 'drink package'. This is a selection of drinks (chosen by the caterer) which will be supplied for a set price per head for a set period of time. This arrangement can be very good for exact budgeting as you know what the price for the drinks will be before you start, as opposed to the 'pay-on-consumption' system. It is also favoured by the caterer as it means less work in calculating the cost. These packages can be useful but bear in mind that the caterer has set their price and will vary the quality of the drinks to be sure they make a profit. You will need to consider any proposal carefully to ensure you are getting the quality you want.

Some general guidelines on drink tray service:

- Make sure there are sufficient serving staff. On-floor staff should be a minimum of one to every 25-30 guests. Caterers will frequently quote this level, but include the bar staff preparing the drinks/washing glasses etc. For a function for 100, you expect to have four waiting staff on the floor but you only get two! Also be careful that the drink-waiting staff do not double up as food-waiting staff. It is a good way to save on the staffing costs but rarely leads to a satisfactory function.
- It is generally best to have the bar in a separate but nearby room so that guests do not approach the bar on a self-service basis. If there is only one large room, consider some screening for the bar.
- The glassware should be of reasonable quality. No one wants their drinks served out of glasses that resemble recycled

Vegemite jars. However, be careful with long-stemmed wine glasses or other shapes that tend to be top heavy. Experienced waiters can have problems balancing these on a tray - university students working part-time have no chance.

- Pre-pouring of drinks can create problems, especially when the ice is placed in the drinks at the pre-pour stage. Surprisingly, this still happens. More ice is added before the drink is served to make it look fresh. Guests receive a very diluted drink - never like the one they make at home. Pre-pouring of the spirit is fine - the addition of the mixer and the ice should only be completed as they go on the tray. Pre-poured beer enlivened with a swizzle stick is never satisfactory.

Experienced waiting staff who receive an order for a drink they do not have on their tray will frequently obtain one from a colleague who is passing or, if they have to return to the bar, will top up their colleague's trays as they pass through the room. This is teamwork that speeds up the drink service.

Drink service at seated functions should be by waiting staff. The arrangement of placing bottles (or carafes) of wine or bottles of beer on the table for guests to serve themselves can only ever be driven by budgetary considerations.

Some general guidelines on table beverage service:

- Wine is the traditional beverage to be served with a meal. However, other beverages should be available and the waiting staff should supply these on order.
- The quality of the wine should be good. There **is** a difference between cask wine or bottled wine at $4.50 a bottle and wine in the higher price range. However, wine does not have to be priced at an absurdly high level. It would take a real connoisseur

to tell the difference between, say, a bottle of wine priced around $12-15 a bottle and something in the $30 range.
- Wine glasses should only be half to two-thirds filled.
- Avoid particularly sweet white wines unless there is a special reason for serving them. Moselle and Gewurztraminer would not be a normal choice.
- For luncheon occasions, select a lighter red wine rather than a full-bodied Shiraz. Keep those for dinners.
- A filled water glass should be provided for each guest. This is even more important these days when everyone is conscious of their alcohol intake. It is acceptable to place a carafe or jug of iced water, preferably with some lemon slices, on the table so that guests may help themselves.

Name Cards/Seating Cards/Place Cards

Name cards are an almost essential feature of a cocktail reception. A cocktail function is usually aimed at allowing as many guests as possible to meet their hosts and one another. They can be very effective networking sessions. This comfortable and free-flowing discussion will not take place unless it is facilitated. Not everyone is confident about walking up to a stranger and starting a conversation. Knowing the person's name and where they come from is a great starting point. It beats an opening discussion on the weather every time.

The most important point with any name card is that the lettering is of sufficient size and clarity to be read without staring or straining. Bold printing of the names is recommended and this is especially important in a room with subdued lighting. The use of coloured or decorated cards often does not help the identification process - black print on a white card may not be that artistically attractive but this format does work.

The addition of the name of the organisation to which the person belongs can be helpful in starting a conversation. The position held does not have to be shown - obtaining that information is one of the starter conversation topics.

An example of a good card is shown below:

> # ANNA STEGGALL
> ## Multipurpose Corporation

With seated functions, guests can be given a seating card on arrival. This is not a name card to be pinned on but a card to be put in the pocket to remind the guest of their table number when they are asked to enter the dining room. The use of a card avoids guests crowding around alphabetical seating plans pinned on an easel display board. By the time they enter the dining room guests have frequently forgotten their table number.

However, unless the guests are well known to one another, it is better to present them with a name card with their table number written on the back of the card (again in large format). This helps ensure that the pre-function drinks (very much like a mini cocktail reception) have all the advantages of making people feel confident and relaxed about speaking to others.

The places at each table are shown with a table card. Ideally, this should be two-sided. The guest's name is shown on the side facing the guest from their seat and their name and organisation is shown on the other side, which can be seen by fellow guests seated at the table. This latter aspect is not essential but, again, it helps in promoting conversation and a feeling of confidence and certainty. The lettering on the table card should be of a size that can easily be read.

At business functions, there is sometimes a list of all guests' names, their organisations and contact telephone numbers provided to all guests as they leave. This is the best time to do it. If it is placed on the tables or on guests' chairs, it is frequently discarded or forgotten. This principle also applies to any mementoes, handouts or glossy material that you would like guests to take with them.

Conduct

The probable success of a function starts before the guests arrive. If guests arrive full of anticipation and feeling relaxed, you are already well ahead. If they feel that they are well looked after during the function, the letters of thanks will arrive (not to you but to your boss, which is always a career enhancer). If they have been unable to find a car park, initially went to the wrong function room and, as a result, arrived late, they are unlikely to be in the best frame of mind.

The following guidelines should assist:

- If the venue is not very well known it may be helpful to include, on a separate piece of paper with the invitation, a map/diagram on how to arrive. This should also provide advice on car parking arrangements.
- Ensure that there are direction signs or staff available to guide guests. Hotels have function boards displayed in the foyer and these are fine. Staff in the foyer of an unfamiliar building to offer directions are always better than an impersonal sign. If you

have to make up your own signs, make sure they are better than a piece of A4 paper stuck on a wall with bluetac or sticky tape!

- Name cards or seating cards should be neatly laid out on a table near the entrance to the function room (but outside it). Look for some space so that guests collecting their name cards do not feel crowded.

- If there is a cloak room, make sure it is attended. If this facility is unavailable, a hanging rack should be provided near the reception desk with adequate coat hangers. These can readily be hired. Ensure any coats, bags or cases left in your care are properly secured during the function.

- Ensure the staff at the name card table are well presented, greet each guest warmly and then assist in finding the guest's name card. They should be well briefed on the function so they can answer any questions on the format as well as the simple questions such as the location of the rest rooms.

- If you use a seating card or a name card with the allocated table number written on the back, there is no need to have an alphabetical seating plan printed and displayed on an easel or noticeboard. However, many guests like to know who will be sitting at their table and a table plan can be helpful. Have it placed to one side in the entry foyer or pre-function drinks area so that it does not cause congestion in the flow of guests into or around the room. Make sure any list is tidily presented and in sufficiently large type size that it can be read easily.

- If the host is at the entrance to the room greeting each guest, it is often helpful to have a staff member in attendance to offer any assistance with names and to ensure a smooth flow of guests. Hosts should not undertake lengthy conversations with guests at this greeting point - just a welcome and a couple of words is sufficient.

- Beverage waiting staff should be inside the door to provide the first drink. Make sure they are not too close to the host otherwise you get a blockage as some guests are choosing their drink and others are banking up behind them.
- When guests depart, staff should be on hand to farewell them and assist with the collection of any cloaks or briefcases that may have been left on arrival. If you are using a portable hanging rack it is a good idea to have that quite prominently positioned near the departure door so that guests are reminded to collect their belongings. This is a lot better than trying to find the owners of the five deserted umbrellas over the next week.

Unfortunately, there are invariably a couple of 'no-shows'. This is quite common at cocktail receptions and causes little problem as there is no seating to worry about. At seated functions, some guests also fail to attend despite any checking that is done in the 48 hours before the function to confirm attendance. What do you do in such cases? The following may help:

- You cannot delay the function for more than five or so minutes waiting for late guests. Invitations to seated functions should have a time frame for arrival - for example, 7.00 pm for 7.30 pm. By 7.25 pm you would be checking who had not arrived and starting to make some plans. If they are seated at the official table, their absence will be noticed and may embarrass the host. In your planning you should identify someone of sufficient status sitting at a lesser table who could be moved to any vacant position on the head table.
- Do not remove vacant place settings immediately in case of very late arrivals. This can best be done with a minimum of fuss by the waiting staff when the entree course is cleared.
- Once the function is under way and no more guests are expected, remove any unclaimed name cards from the table in the

foyer. Departing guests should not be able to peruse the name cards to see who 'failed to show'.

A hospitality function check list is attached at Appendix C.

For Further Information

- Contact the appropriate protocol office listed in Appendix A.

* * *

A sister-state relationship was established between Victoria and Jiangsu Province in China. The final discussions and the signing of the agreement took place during a visit to Jiangsu by the Premier of Victoria. As this was the first visit, the Premier's delegation was feted by the Chinese hosts, including formal banquets and lots of sightseeing. The Chinese hosts were trying very hard to impress. The delegation was told that there was a special treat for lunch on the day they were due to leave.

The lunch was a small affair hosted by the Governor of the Province in his private dining room. The special treat was that it was a Western-style meal. The Chinese chef had probably never cooked such a meal before and had followed recipes in Mrs Beaton's Family Cookbook of 1940. The delegation's hearts (and stomachs) sank as they saw that each dish was generous in proportion but also that the meal comprised eight courses! Honour had to be defended and everyone made a valiant effort. The meal was still being enjoyed 48 hours later.

The idea was commendable but it does suggest that it is best to stick to what you know and do well.

INVITATIONS

Styles of Invitations

Invitations are the means of asking individuals to attend a function. With the advancement of technology, they now take many forms. They vary from the telephone call to personal friends to attend a private dinner party, to the traditional formal-printed white cards. The form of invitation should be appropriate to the intended style of the function as this can influence the guests in their acceptance and their anticipation of the event. If you send a formal invitation, this indicates that the event itself will tend towards formality and an expectation is established in the guest's mind.

A formal invitation does not have to be in the form of the traditional printed white card. It may be handwritten if there are only a small number of personal guests, or it may be printed on appropriately sized, good-quality corporate notepaper. What is important is to decide the style of function that you want and have the invitation, in both wording and appearance, convey your message.

For less formal functions, the style of the invitation can be whatever you want. There is a huge range of sizes and formats which is only limited by your imagination or that of your graphic designer. It can be useful to keep those invitations you receive which caught your eye or encouraged you to attend. They can be useful to spark ideas when you have to prepare one of your own. Bear in mind that the more colourful and intricate the invitation is, especially with cut-outs and folding, the cost increases quite dramatically.

Whatever the occasion, the traditional white card is always acceptable. It is generally 15 cm x 11 cm in size, although it can be bigger. It may be gold-edged. It may have rounded edges. The invitation is printed on the face of the card and administrative details such as a map or parking arrangements may be printed on the reverse. If the organisation has a coat of arms or distinctive logo, this is normally printed on the top centre of the card. Such a device should be printed in colour to differentiate it from the black wording.

The essential information which should be shown on every invitation, irrespective of the style used, is:

- The name of the host and the position held (avoid issuing invitations in the name of a company or corporation - every host has a face)
- The name(s) of the invitee(s) (see below on Writing of Invitations)
- The type of function (luncheon, dinner, cocktail reception, product launch)
- The purpose or reason or name of the event
- The location (including the name of the room in a hotel, and the full street address)
- The date
- The time (it is helpful to give a time range for a seated event such as dinner - for example, 7 for 7.30 pm)
- The dress (if formal, the male attire is normally the only dress stated - for example, black tie)
- The date for responses (RSVP date), together with a name/address/e-mail for the reply (see details below)

The catch phrase for essential information is: "What - When - Where - Why."

Compiling a Guest List for an Official Function

This should be tackled as soon as a function is proposed and before the venue and the form of the function are confirmed. Initially, it may appear very clear who should be invited but it is often useful to clarify in your mind the purpose of the function and what is trying to be achieved. When that is clear, you can think about whom could play a part in that success. Rather than thinking of guest names, it is helpful to start with a list of guest categories to be sure you have 'covered the field'. Next, you should put some planning numbers next to the categories which will give you an idea of the size of the function. At this stage, you will need to decide whether spouses will be included. Which categories are included will depend on the purpose of the function. To spark your thoughts, the following very general categories (far from comprehensive) could be considered:

Cabinet Ministers	Leader of the Opposition
Parliamentarians	Municipal representatives
Church leaders	The judiciary
Emergency services	Multicultural organisations
Business organisations	Diplomatic/consular representatives
Community organisations	Host or guest of honour's personal guests
Government officers	Trade union representatives
Education organisations	News media

Writing of Invitations

It is traditional for the names of guests to be written on the invitation by hand in black ink. This shows a degree of personal commitment by the host.

There are now a number of computer packages available which print the invitation cards and also insert the name of the guest using a script font. The packages also use the name/address database to produce the envelopes, place cards, name cards, guest lists and seating plans. These packages are now in wide use by organisations issuing a lot of invitations, including government and some Vice-Regal establishments. They have growing acceptance, even by the purists. However, a distinctive script font must be used for the invitee's name. The use of a typeface similar in style and size to that used in the body of the invitation is not acceptable.

The name of the guest is all that is written on the invitation. Honours, decorations and other award initials, which are customarily shown after a person's name, are not written on the invitation cards. They are shown on the envelope.

Some commercial organisations use what may be described as 'bulk invitations' where they are not personalised but contain a phrase similar to 'This invitation admits two people'. These are impersonal and show little thought has gone into their preparation. They are only slightly better than a newspaper advertisement.

Style of Writing Names on Invitations

There is great flexibility on how the names are written on invitations. Courtesy should be the guideline. Names or official appointments may be used. Some examples are:

- Mr and Mrs J Brown
- Mr and Mrs John Brown
- The Honourable John and Mrs Brown
- The Hon J and Mrs S Brown
- Professor and Mrs John Brown
- Dr S and Mr J Brown
- The Prime Minister and Mrs Brown
- The Mayor and Mayoress of Scheyville
- Judge and Mrs J Brown

With less formal invitations, a more relaxed and informal style can be used. Examples are:

- John and Sally Brown
- Tara Wycliffe and Alan Moseley
- Damon and Jackie

When it is intended to invite husbands and wives, every effort should be made to find out whether a principal guest is married and write the invitation accordingly. Some long-married people refuse to accept an invitation if they are invited as Mr John Brown and partner.

However, it is not always possible to obtain this information. These days the term 'partner' indicates a degree of commitment between the two people. If this is known then this term can be used. Where there is any doubt, the term 'guest' may be more appropriate although it is not as warm a term as 'partner'. A decision for the host!

Widows

The traditional position on addressing widows has been to use their former husband's initials. This convention is now rarely followed and the majority of widows now prefer to use their own initials or given name. This would be the recommended course of action unless there is a known preference for the traditional style.

Divorced and Separated Guests

Where a marriage has broken down or been dissolved, the female may retain her married name (often the case where school-aged children are involved), or may revert to her own family name. The form of address should always follow the known preference.

Envelopes

There was a social convention that envelopes containing invitations should be addressed to the female member of any marriage. With the more complex arrangements of personal partnerships these days this procedure is now rarely followed.

It is probably best to address the envelope to the principal guest at that person's business address. This is because most busy business executives have their personal assistant or secretary arrange their diaries as opposed to the spouse at home. This was the reason for the traditional practice of addressing the invitations to the wife at the home address.

Invitation envelopes should show the honorifics and post-nominals of honours and awards of the recipient. However, academic post-nominals are not normally shown. Examples are:

- Mr J D Smith AM
- Professor Jackie Jones AO
- Sir Ronald Green AC OBE

If you wish to address the envelope to both recipients (and this would normally only be done for more informal invitations addressed to home), the style should be:

- Mr and Mrs J D Smith
- Sir Ronald and Lady Green

Post-nominals are not used in these cases. It is wrong to address an envelope:

- Mr and Mrs J D Smith AM

Timing and Format of the Dispatch of Invitations

Despite the growth of alternative means of communication, invitations should be sent by Australia Post mail unless they are very informal and are sent to a group of close friends. Any invitation sent by facsimile or e-mail is regarded as second-rate and is likely to be treated as such.

The timing of the dispatch of invitations is important. In today's hectic business environment, diaries start to fill up about one month ahead. If invitations arrive two months in advance, they may be overlooked or responses may be slow, as there is uncertainty about other engagements that may arrive. Whether we like it or not, people do work on the principle of 'waiting for a better offer'. The ideal window of opportunity is for the invitation to arrive, by post, somewhere between four and five weeks before the event. This lead time is not always possible but it should be the aim.

Replies to Invitations (RSVPs)

The term RSVP is the accepted abbreviation requesting a response to the invitation. It is an anagram of the French phrase 'respondez s'il vous plais', which literally means 'would you please reply'.

The date on which a reply is requested should be selected to allow sufficient time for planning of the event to proceed smoothly but early enough to allow any guests who have not responded to be followed up by telephone. The date requested for a seated occasion would normally be earlier than that required for a cocktail reception where guests will be standing. About a week before a cocktail party event would be normal.

Where there is some doubt about the acceptance by all guests and it is important to maintain a minimum number of attendees, the RSVP date may be earlier. This will allow the hosts to use a 'second eleven' guest list without making it appear too obvious to those who were not included in the original list. An original RSVP at least two weeks before the event would be required if this ploy were to be used.

While the issue of invitations should be by mail, the acceptance process should be made as easy as possible for the guests. Facsimile and e-mail responses are quite acceptable and, with business invitations, are generally welcomed. However, not all guests may have access to these means of communication and it is important to allow alternatives. Some suggestions are:

- Reply Slip A reply slip included with the invitation is the preferred method of receiving responses. The replies can be held in the office until there is a suitable time for the designated member of staff to process them. There is a written record of the acceptance or decline, and a request for return personal details lets you check the correct spelling of names and details of titles for use on seating or name cards. Additionally, it allows you to update your database with correct addresses and post-nominals. You can also seek advice on requests for such things as vegetarian meals. The reply slip should show both mail and facsimile addresses for responses. Use a light-coloured paper as dark backgrounds will not transmit satisfactorily by facsimile. A stiff reply card will require photocopying before it can be successfully transmitted by facsimile and is not necessary - a good quality paper reply slip is fine.
- e-Mail e-Mail is almost universally available within the Australian business community and is a growing means of communication. The reply slip should still be used but include an e-mail address if you wish to offer this response alternative.
- Telephone If it is a comparatively small event and there are not a number of functions being run concurrently, responses can be collected by providing a specific telephone number, together with the name of the person who should be contacted. This system may also have to be used where the lead time before the function is short. It has the disadvantages of possible errors in recording acceptances (especially where responses are taken by

different members of staff) and can cause frustration to guests if the telephone is frequently engaged. It can also be costly in staff time.

- <u>Formal Response</u> On occasions a formal written response may be requested although these are becoming less common. Vice-Regal functions are now normally accompanied by a reply slip. However, some wedding invitations request a formal response. A suggested format is shown at Appendix D.

For Further Information

- Contact the appropriate protocol office shown in Appendix A.

* * *

During a visit by The Queen a garden party was arranged at Government House. The invitation categories included a large number of senior citizens, but the numbers that could be invited were very tight. Shortly after the invitations were issued, a telephone call was received from Gracie Smith who explained that her husband was unwell and would not be able to attend. Would it be acceptable for her to be accompanied by her close friend Vera Jones? This was agreed to and the guest list adjusted. Two days before the garden party Gracie rang again and explained that her husband had amazingly recovered and now would be able to attend. However, as her friend Vera had been looking forward to the function so much and had bought a new hat, would it still be possible for her to attend? This was agreed to. "And her husband Jack?" asked Gracie.

Never underestimate a senior citizen!

TOASTS

Toasts are the traditional way of paying respect to a person, organisation or an ideal. They are generally related to a hospitality function such as a dinner, luncheon or cocktail reception where guests will consume beverages. This section deals with loyal and formal toasts. It does not deal with an informal toast such as that to the bride and groom or a toast in a business situation which may relate to the continued success of a project. These toasts normally occur at the end of a speech or may be proposed extemporaneously.

The following general guidelines may be helpful:

- Toasts may be drunk in alcoholic or non-alcoholic beverages.
- Guests stand to honour a toast unless there are physical reasons which prohibit them from doing so. If the toast is to a person who is present, that person does not rise to drink the toast.
- The toast to a country takes the form of a toast to the Head of State of the country concerned.
- Although smoking at a meal or in a confined entertainment space is now a rarity in Australia, it is the custom that smoking is not permitted until after the toasts have been completed.
- At dinners arranged by some organisations, such as the Australian Defence Force, there may be an established precedent whereby the toasts are not proposed until the meal has been completed and the table cleared. Where there is no such precedent, a toast may be offered at any appropriate and convenient stage of the function. In practical terms, it is probably best to have the Loyal Toast early in the order of proceedings after the guests have settled but not become too relaxed. At a dinner, after the first course is usually a good time.
- As mentioned elsewhere, a dinner/luncheon format that has gained in popularity in recent times is to conduct all the formalities before the meal is served (the Chinese format). If this format is used, it is best to have the Loyal Toast at the very beginning before any speeches. However, don't forget to pre-pour the beverages!

- In the case of a formal toast to a Head of State, the toast should not be immediately preceded by a speech. The Loyal Toast and any associated toasts to other countries should stand alone.

The Loyal Toast in Australia

The Loyal Toast is a toast that citizens of all countries use to honour their Head of State. It is a means of displaying the loyalty and allegiance that citizens have to their country. In Australia, the standard form of the Loyal Toast is:

> *Her Majesty The Queen of Australia*

During the visit to Australia by The Queen in March 2000, a variation to the standard form of toast was used with The Queen's approval. This form of Loyal Toast was used in The Queen's presence throughout Australia at all functions where a toast was proposed. This was not the first time that this form of toast had been used - it had been the form of toast at formal functions at both Government House and Parliament House in Canberra for some years. It is probably the result of the increasing debate over the constitutional arrangements in Australia during the late 1990s. This alternative form of Loyal Toast is:

> *The Queen and the People of Australia*

Either form of Loyal Toast may be used at the discretion of the host.

Proposing a Loyal Toast

The general form for proposing and honouring a Loyal Toast is as follows:

- Ascertain that all guests have a glass of beverage available.

- The attention of the guests is obtained by the Master of Ceremonies (or the host).
- When there is silence, the person proposing the Loyal Toast (usually the host) rises and, with glass in hand, says:

   Ladies and Gentlemen, I give you the Toast to Her Majesty The Queen of Australia

   or

   Ladies and Gentlemen, please join me in the Toast to The Queen and the People of Australia

- The guests rise and take up their glasses.
- The host then offers the toast by saying:

   The Queen of Australia

   or

   The Queen and the People of Australia

- The guests repeat the form of the toast the host has used and the toast is honoured by all guests (including the host) taking a sip from their glasses.
- The host and guests resume their seats.

The preamble words to the toast shown above can be varied to suit the wishes of the person proposing the toast. The following introductory phrases are all acceptable:

   Would you join me in the toast to....

   Please charge your glasses for the toast to....

   I propose the toast to....

The phrase *God Bless Her* is sometimes said by one or two guests after the Loyal Toast has been honoured and before guests sit down. This is most common at ex-service functions. It is not part of the procedure and is an informal custom which is falling into disuse.

Proposing a Loyal Toast with Musical Honours

This form of Loyal Toast is less common and can only occur when an appropriate live band (generally a military or brass band) is present to play the National Anthem. Recorded music should not be used.

The general form of the toast is the same as described previously. When guests have risen to their feet the band plays the Australian National Anthem (*Advance Australia Fair*) in full. At the conclusion of the playing of the anthem, the host offers the toast and it is honoured as previously explained.

Some guests may sing the National Anthem when it is played. If someone starts singing all other guests normally join in. This is perfectly acceptable.

As this form of toast is rarely used, it can cause confusion with guests attempting to honour the toast while the band is playing. Rehearsal with the band and the person proposing the toast is recommended.

The full first verse of *Advance Australia Fair* should be played. Some bandmasters incorrectly suggest that the 'short form' of the National Anthem be played. There is no short form. What they are referring to is the Vice-Regal Salute which is played as a salute to the Governor-General or the Governor. This comprises the first four and last four bars of *Advance Australia Fair*. The Vice-Regal Salute is never played as part of a Loyal Toast.

Proposing More than One Loyal Toast

At a function where there is a guest of honour from another country, it may be courteous to propose a toast to the Head of State of that country but it is not obligatory.

This second toast follows the same format as that previously described for the Loyal Toast. At the conclusion of the Loyal Toast to The Queen (in whichever format) and before the guests are seated, the host would propose a toast to the Head of State of the guest of honour. This follows the procedure previously described.

It is important that the correct form of toast to the foreign Head of State is used. This is best ascertained by asking the guest of honour or one of her personal staff beforehand. Alternatively, the appropriate diplomatic/consular post could be consulted.

Should there be two guests of honour, it may be possible to have a third Loyal Toast following this format. However, three toasts would be the practical limit before the procedure becomes repetitive and the dignity of the occasion is lost.

When there are a number of foreign guests present and it is appropriate for their Heads of State to be recognised, the internationally accepted form of toast following the Loyal Toast to The Queen (in whichever format) is:

The Heads of State of Other Countries Here Represented

The Toast to the Queen (in whichever format) precedes the other toasts. There are exceptions to this general rule when the foreign Head of State is present and also at National Day celebrations. These are described later.

There may be occasions when the foreign countries represented are all Commonwealth countries which recognise The Queen as Head of State- for example, the UK, Canada, New Zealand and Papua New Guinea. To propose a number of toasts to the same person but under different titles would be farcical. The one Loyal Toast in such a situation should be:

> *Her Majesty The Queen*
>
> or
>
> *Her Majesty The Queen, Head of the Commonwealth*

Loyal Toasts when the Head of State of a Foreign Country is Present

It is unlikely that this situation will arise other than in the most formal of occasions. A full reconnaissance and rehearsal of the proceedings will have been conducted by government protocol officers and representatives of the visiting Head of State.

Toast details will be discussed and agreed to during the preparatory phases of the visit. These can be complicated and are not described here.

Toasts at National Day Functions

Diplomatic and consular representatives frequently hold functions to honour their country's National Day. These functions are normally either a lunchtime or a late afternoon cocktail reception.

The focal point of the function is an exchange of Loyal Toasts to the Head of State of the country concerned and The Queen of Australia. As this function is a special recognition of the foreign country concerned, the Loyal Toast to that country's Head of State is proposed first, followed by the Loyal Toast to The Queen. This procedure is not always followed and, at some consular functions, the Loyal Toast to The Queen is proposed first. This may be because the arrangements followed by the foreign country vary from ours. This is not a matter of great concern.

The Loyal Toast to the foreign country's Head of State is proposed by the guest of honour who has been invited by the head of post to propose the toast. This is normally the Chief of Protocol at diplomatic functions in Canberra. At consular functions in the States, a Minister or a parliamentary secretary of the State government usually proposes the toast. The return Loyal Toast to The Queen of Australia is proposed by the diplomatic/consular head of post.

The guest of honour should ensure that the form of toast to the foreign Head of State is correct by seeking prior advice from the head of the diplomatic/consular post.

At National Day functions, there are only two Loyal Toasts. Although other countries' diplomatic/consular representatives may be present as guests, their Heads of State are not recognised by a Loyal Toast.

It is traditional that, at National Day functions, there should be no speeches in support of the Loyal Toasts. However, this is not always observed at consular functions. The head of post frequently welcomes guests and these comments can expand into quite a lengthy speech during which the head of post reviews the year in their country or speaks on the development of the relationship between the foreign country and Australia. To respond in kind, the guest of honour frequently speaks on the value of the relationship to Australia.

Although the following procedure may not be strictly followed in every case, it is a guide:

- Silence is called for by the Master of Ceremonies.
- The host announces the guest of honour.
- The guest of honour proposes the Loyal Toast to the foreign Head of State.

Ladies and Gentlemen, I give you the toast to His Majesty the King of Thailand

- The guest of honour offers the toast by saying:

The King

- The guests repeat the form of toast the guest of honour has used and the toast is honoured.

- The host immediately says:

Ladies and Gentlemen, I give you the toast to Her Majesty The Queen of Australia

- The host offers the toast by saying:

The Queen of Australia

- The guests repeat the form of toast the host has used and the toast is honoured.

For Further Information

- Contact the appropriate protocol office shown in Appendix A.

* * *

The chairman of a large and respected law firm held a major formal dinner for senior executives and major clients and their spouses each year. As he had served as an officer in the Army, the format for the dinner followed military lines with the Loyal Toast being drunk at the end of the dinner after the table had been cleared of all but the port glasses. He also followed the military tradition of the toast being proposed by the most junior officer. A few weeks before the function, the junior was summoned to the chairman's office and given his instructions, including some emphasis on how important it was that the toast be handled correctly. The young man rehearsed his lines ad nauseam to make sure that all went well. On the night the chairman called for silence and announced the

Loyal Toast. When everyone was standing the young man, in a loud and clear voice, proposed the toast: "Ladies and Quentlemen, The Gents."

History does not record the results of the inevitable meeting in the chairman's office next morning.

Chapter 3

Ceremonial Matters

CEREMONY

Ceremonial plays a part in all our lives at particular times. On the personal side, there is a ceremony for weddings, baptisms and funerals. The ceremony varies in style and formality depending on individual wishes but it is still a form of ceremony. This section will not attempt to cover every form of ceremony but will focus on some common elements that should be considered, as well as some aspects that may be unfamiliar to many. Some general guidelines are:

- Make the ceremony appear as natural as possible. Apply the KISS principle (Keep It Simple, Stupid).
- Avoid contrived situations.
- A long ceremony is usually not a particularly good ceremony. As always, quality is more important than quantity.

- Don't be unduly constrained by historical precedent. There is not much done today in the same way as it was 20 years ago.
- All ceremonial activities require a well-conceived plan, documented in a running sheet, with a detailed briefing for the participants.
- All ceremonial requires rehearsal.

Official Openings

Opening ceremonies for a conference or similar activities usually take the form of an official party being seated on a raised dais in front of an invited audience.

In the case of a conference, a professional conference organiser may have been employed to make all the arrangements but, professional or not, they require supervision. They are often more interested in the 'bells and whistles' aspect of the opening and overlook some of the principles of good ceremony.

Some matters to consider are:

- Will the audience be seated or standing? Seating is normal for indoor ceremonies. The duration of the ceremony and the age of the participants may be a consideration.
- The official dais should not look too crowded. Making it bigger is not necessarily the answer. If there are a large number of important persons, one alternative is to seat the less-important dignitaries in the front row of the audience. It may be possible for these persons to have gathered previously with the official party in a separate room for refreshments and then precede the official party into the auditorium. Alternatively, they could be invited to join the official party for refreshments after the opening ceremony. If spouses are involved, they may be seated

in the front row of the audience with only the principals being seated on the dais.

- As a guide, one chair requires a minimum area of one square metre. This gives an uncrowded appearance from the front and just allows enough space for movement between any subsequent rows.

- There will frequently be only one guest of honour. Other persons on the dais may be senior office-bearers from the organisation concerned. In this case they would be seated in their order of importance working outwards from the centre where the host and the guest of honour are seated. If there are other official guests on the dais, they should be seated alternately with members of the organisation in order of importance.

- If the official party is to sit behind a table on the dais, the Australian or State flags should not be used as tablecloths or as masking on the front of the table, dais or platform. It is important that the front of any tables are masked (as it is with the dais) but plain material should be used.

- The positioning of the lectern is important. If it is placed in the centre of the dais it will block the audience's view of the guest of honour (and vice versa) and will also make it difficult for the speaker to acknowledge the guest of honour without turning away from the audience. Consideration should be given to having the lectern at one side of the dais with a second lectern on the other side to give a balanced appearance. This second lectern could be used by the master of ceremonies. It also provides an alternative should the microphone on the main dais fail (remember Murphy's Law - if something can go wrong, it will).

- If the news media are expected to attend, some arrangements will need to be made for television and still photographers. Their view must be a good one without interrupting the view of the audience. If it is not good they will either not use the pictures or they will move to a position which suits them (which will almost certainly not suit you). You should also consider the background decoration. Reflecting surfaces, a location in front of a window and certain colours may not be suitable. It is best to seek advice if you are not familiar with the pictorial media requirements.

- The seats on the dais should have name cards placed either on the seats themselves or on the floor in front of the seats. The type must be large enough to be read from a distance and they should be secured with adhesive tape or bluetac. The slightest breeze, even in an auditorium, could cause chaos. Even if the seating is simple, the names are still necessary. The dais layout never looks the same as the seating plan which was memorised two minutes before.

- In the case of Vice-Regal occasions an aide, personal assistant and/or secretary will normally be in attendance. If there is more than one, only the aide needs to be seated on the dais. He or she should be seated in a second row immediately behind their principal. Should there be insufficient space for a second row, they may be seated at the end of the official seating but this should be avoided. An aide from Government House will contact the host some weeks before the event to discuss the arrangements. If a Vice-Regal salute is to be played by a live band or by recorded music, this is not played until the Vice-Regal representative and all members of the official party are standing in front of their seats. It is **not** played as they enter the auditorium. If some entry music is required, use a fanfare or something similar.

- There has been a growing trend in recent years to include a welcoming ceremony by the traditional owners of Australia in opening and similar ceremonies. There is quite a wide range of such ceremonies and, through discussion, a format which suits your overall ceremonial arrangements can usually be found.

Some diagramatic layouts are suggested below:

OPENING CEREMONIES

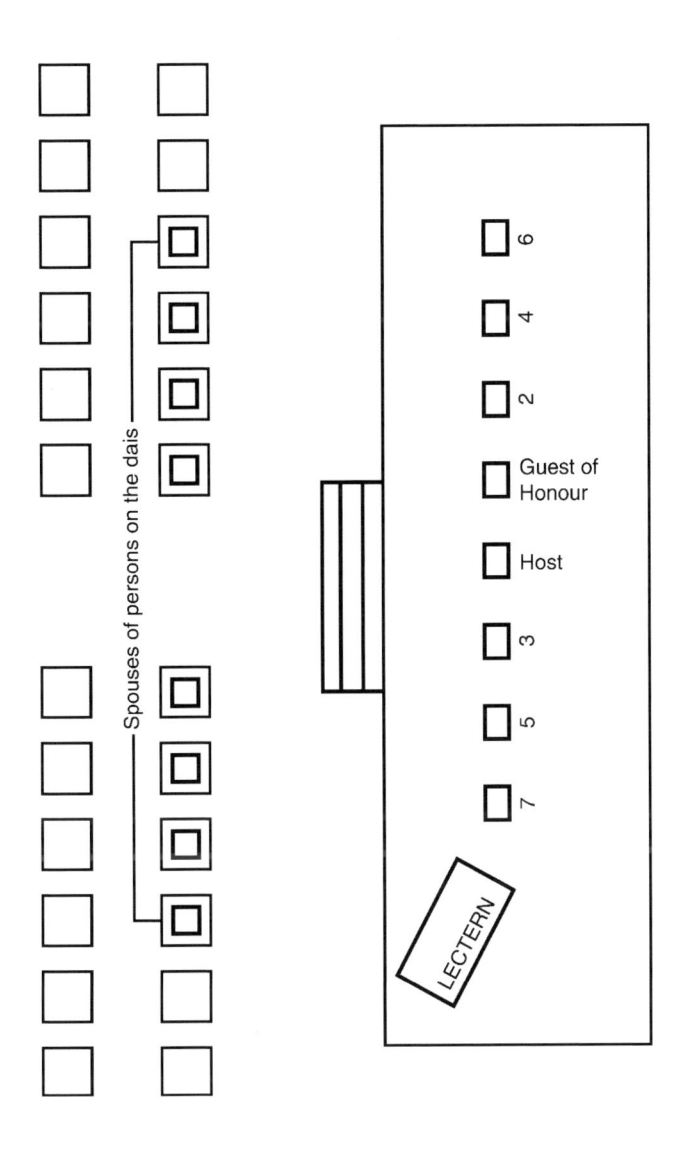

WHO'S WHO GUIDE TO PROTOCOL

OPENING CEREMONIES - VICE REGAL OCCASIONS

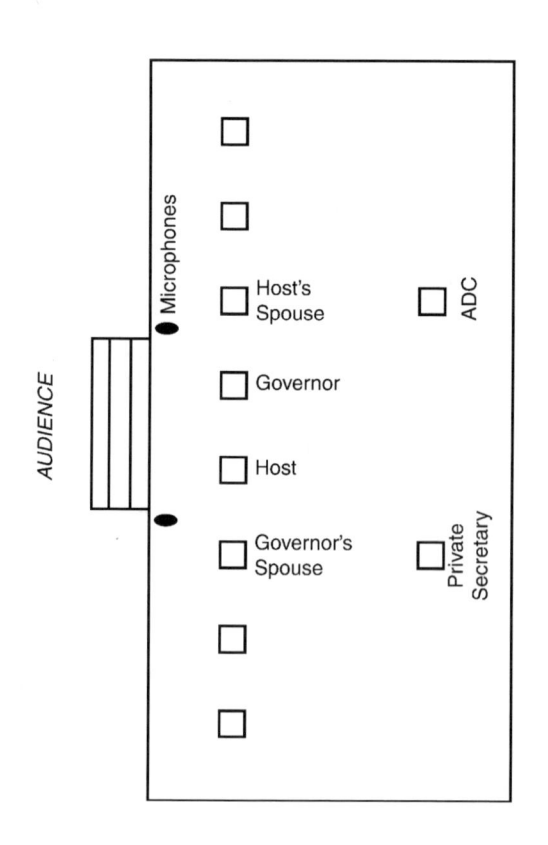

OPENING CEREMONIES - SEVERAL VIP GUESTS

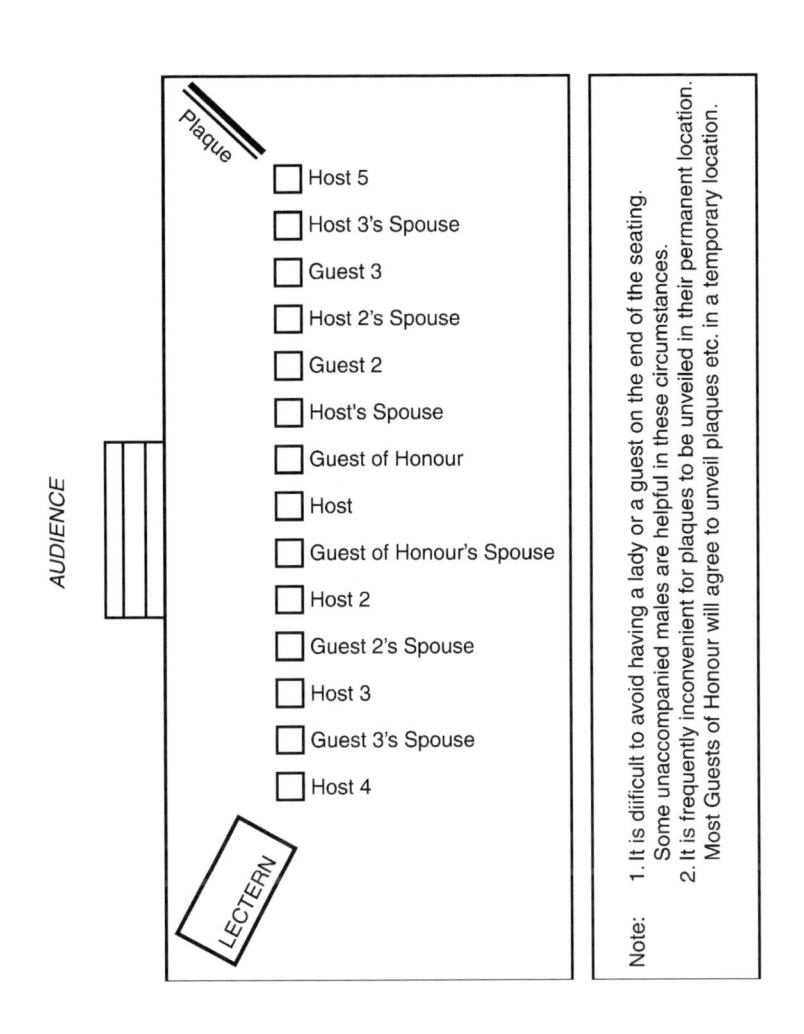

Plaque

- Host 5
- Host 3's Spouse
- Guest 3
- Host 2's Spouse
- Guest 2
- Host's Spouse
- Guest of Honour
- Host
- Guest of Honour's Spouse
- Host 2
- Guest 2's Spouse
- Host 3
- Guest 3's Spouse
- Host 4

AUDIENCE

LECTERN

Note:
1. It is difficult to avoid having a lady or a guest on the end of the seating. Some unaccompanied males are helpful in these circumstances.
2. It is frequently inconvenient for plaques to be unveiled in their permanent location. Most Guests of Honour will agree to unveil plaques etc. in a temporary location.

In the case of the opening of a construction such as a building, a bridge or similar facility, what will be the physical act that marks the opening? There are many options but some comments on favourite procedures are:

- If a plaque is to be unveiled it may not be convenient to hold the opening ceremony in front of the final location of the plaque. In this case, the plaque should be fixed to a solid stand and placed in an appropriate position on the dais. It should be covered by plain material (not a flag) and the unveiling mechanism should have only one cord visible to be pulled. Alternatively, the curtain may be pulled aside by hand but make sure, whichever method is used, that the plaque is fully exposed when the covering is pulled back. An alternative is to have the covering attached to a rod which can be simply lifted off a couple of hooks. Unveiling devices can be hired from major hospitality hiring firms and this professional help is usually worthwhile. This is a favourite photographic shot so make sure the media is able to cover the action without replays, which not all guests of honour will agree to perform.

- Unveiling of statues or similar large objects is usually difficult and untidy. No matter how it is wrapped, the unveiling device seems to fail or the covering material gets caught on some protuberance. Again, plain material and not a flag should be used. No real clues here other than to say that trial and error during rehearsals will help.

- Cutting a ribbon is another popular ceremonial opening method. The ribbon needs to be brightly coloured and of sufficient width to make it look substantial. It should be reasonably taut and this may need some last-minute adjustment - the taut ribbon of two minutes ago has a nasty habit of sagging when exposed to the sun. The cutting instrument needs to be sharp. If more than one person is to perform the act, the decision needs to be made whether to obtain a large pair of ceremonial scissors that all can place a hand on or whether several pairs of conventional scissors are provided. The latter is the normal case, but if one snipper is quicker than the others, they can be denied a cut!

- Turning the key in the door to open a building is less common these days. It does not make much of a ceremony as the guest of honour invariably has his back turned to the audience and the media find it hard to cover the shot. Trying to take a photograph from the other side of a locked glass door rarely gives good results.
- Triggering an action, such as switching on Christmas lights or activating a fountain, by pressing a button or pulling a lever adjacent to the dais, is technologically possible but, as Sir Humphrey Appleby would say, such a choice would be a courageous decision. If this procedure is to be used it is best to have a dummy/ceremonial lever or button on the dais with the actual activation being done manually by a qualified technician from a properly wired remote location. Portable radio communication may be required if the operator cannot see the act of simulated activation.
- A wet-weather plan should be devised. This can vary from going ahead with the fine weather proposal with everyone holding umbrellas or it may require some major alternative arrangements.

Tree Planting

Tree plantings are quite popular as they leave a lasting legacy of the occasion and are environmentally friendly. The normal procedure is to have the tree already well planted with a small pile of loose earth adjacent to the new tree. The tree should be of reasonable size (about 1.5 to 2 metres) and not look like an insignificant twig.

The guest of honour is invited to add some earth with a ceremonial shovel and tramp it down with their foot. The ceremonial shovel does not need to have a chromed blade, but it should be freshly painted, the handle should be varnished and any commercial labels removed. Any associated plaque recording the occasion can be added after the ceremony.

It is wise to have some spare trees available. On one occasion, when The Queen planted a tree, it had to be replaced by the municipality concerned six times in the first 48 hours. There are a lot of light-fingered residents claiming that the tree in their backyard was planted by The Queen!

Laying a Wreath

The laying of wreaths is generally related to ex-service ceremonies or some other form of remembrance service. If asked to lay a wreath you should seek guidance from the organisers on the format they require. The following general points should be considered:

- Make sure you are clear who is providing the wreath - the organisers or the wreath-layer.
- A wreath should be a wreath, not a sheath or basket of flowers.
- The wreath should be made of fresh flowers/greenery. The wreaths made of plastic leaves are a poor substitute. They also have no weight and blow away in the slightest breeze.
- The colour of the flowers should be left to the florist to choose so that the freshest seasonal flowers available are used, unless there is some particular significance in colours for the occasion. Not all florists are as experienced in making wreaths as they would like to believe. It would not hurt to remind them to avoid flowers that shed their petals easily.
- Make sure that there is a card on the wreath stating the name of the individual or the organisation on whose behalf the wreath

is laid. A specially prepared card is better than one provided by the florist.

- The general format for laying a wreath when wearing civilian clothes is:
    - carrying the wreath, and without wearing any head-dress in the case of males, walk at normal pace towards the wreath-laying point and stop about 2 metres away.
    If you have to wear head-dress for medical reasons, it should be removed before laying the wreath and not replaced until you move away from the wreath-laying position.
    - pause for about 2-3 seconds and then place the wreath.
    - Step back about 2 metres and remain with your head bowed for about five seconds. You may wish to place your clenched right hand over your heart during this period.
    - Turn about and return to your place at normal walking pace.

Taking a Salute

A VIP may be asked to take the salute from a dais as marching, mounted or motorised elements of a parade pass by. The format and content of the parade should indicate what is expected of the dignitary.

Military and similar parades by uniformed bodies or emergency service groups have a certain disciplined ceremony about them and the participants take some action to recognise the dignitary taking the salute. The participants either salute, turn their heads towards the reviewing officer or take some other ceremonial action that requires some dignified response from the VIP. Advice should be sought from the parade organisers on the format proposed. The following matters should be considered:

- The reviewing officer should stand alone at the front of the dais with any other members of the official party standing a metre or so behind. This may be modified where there is established precedent, such as an Anzac Day parade, where the duration of the march past is more than three hours. In such cases, the reviewing officer is normally seated.
- As each group passes and pays its compliments, it should be acknowledged by a nod of the head. If the VIP is male and a hat is worn, this should be removed as each group passes and then replaced before the next group approaches when the procedure is repeated. This is a good way of returning the compliments, even if a hat is not normally worn.
- It is not appropriate to chat to other members of the official party while compliments are being paid. The VIP should give undivided attention to the passing participants.
- If the weather is inclement, the VIP will win lots of 'brownie points' if he or she suffers the same weather conditions as the participants rather than sheltering under cover.

Conditions are somewhat different for a community celebratory parade which is comparatively unstructured. Formal compliments are not paid and it is difficult to remain serious when the participants are made up of marching girls, community groups, clowns and colourful floats. In this case, a more relaxed approach should be taken with the VIP recognising each group with a smile and a wave. However, it is important that the VIP pays attention to each group rather than chatting with others on the dais.

Foundation Stones

Foundation stones were popular in the late 19th and early 20th centuries but they are now rarely used. The speed of current building techniques means that a building is completed within a comparatively short time. Foundation stones have lost their relevance.

Plaques

A plaque is designed to record a significant happening and to last as long as the building or object to which it is attached. Outdoor plaques should be cast metal. The much cheaper styles, which can be made up very quickly by laser-engraving on metal-coloured plastic sheets, quickly become discoloured and fall apart if used outside. Such plaques may be suitable for inside use but they do lack the substance and permanent appearance of cast metal.

Some plaques unveiled in the earlier part of the 20th century can look like the front page of the *Sydney Morning Herald*. There are so many names of the municipal councillors, town clerk, shire engineer and others that the reason for the plaque is virtually lost. It may have been important at the time but has little relevance to a reader today. However, it does prove the point that everyone likes to see their name in print - if possible, for posterity!

The modern approach is to keep plaques simple. A good example of a plaque to mark the opening of a facility is:

> THE PIONEERS STAND
> WAS OFFICIALLY OPENED BY
> **THE HON DAVID GILLETT, AM, MP**
> MINISTER FOR SPORT
> ON 15 MARCH 2001
> *
> A JOINT CENTENARY OF FEDERATION PROJECT OF THE
> TASMANIAN GOVERNMENT AND THE CITY OF DRUMKIND

The following guidelines may be useful:

- The size of the plaque should be aesthetically pleasing to the eye and appear in proportion to the surface to which it is attached.
- The same style of lettering should be used throughout, although the size may be varied to give emphasis.
- A badge, logo or coat of arms of the organisation concerned may be placed at the top of the plaque.
- Leave the production of the plaque until the last possible moment, especially if politicians are involved. Some VIPs have a habit of becoming unavailable and a new plaque only adds to the expense. Should a last-minute cancellation occur, the opening ceremony should be restructured to avoid the plaque unveiling element unless you want the undoubted publicity of an incorrectly named plaque!

For Further Information

- Contact the appropriate protocol office listed in Appendix A.

* * *

In 1986, the Pope visited Australia and as he came into Melbourne from the airport in the 'Popemobile', people were lining the route all the way. As the motorcade turned into the top end of Swanston Street, there was a tunnel of people to drive through. We could see one group standing out above the others as it was standing on the tray of a flatbed truck. As we got closer you could see that they were all females. We could tell this as they were dressed only in bras and G-strings or something similar. They enthusiastically welcomed the Pope as he drove by and he returned the greeting. As we drove past them, we saw that they had come from a terrace house whose facade was painted red and was decorated with a red light. It had a very appropriate name board displayed. It read 'Heavenly Bodies'.

FORMS OF ADDRESS

Australian Practice

Australia does not have a complicated system of titles such as exists in other countries - for example, the peerage in the United Kingdom. However, it would be true to say, in general terms, that the number of formal titles and methods of address have become less complicated worldwide in recent times.

The key to the whole matter of addressing someone, whether it be in writing or face to face, is courtesy. However, there are some conventions and these should be followed wherever there is any doubt on any preferred form of address.

In face-to-face conversations, the aim is to appear and sound natural. It is always better to revert to the safe and sure "Sir" or "Madam" rather than become tongue-tied and perplexed with a difficult or complex title, possibly in a language other than English, that you are not used to saying and which does not slip naturally off your tongue.

Some conventional forms of address which may be helpful are shown at Appendix E.

Some readers may feel that the conventions shown in the appendix are not complete. For example, in the form of address to a Mayor, there is no mention of the title 'Your Worship'. This is one of the titles that became obsolescent in Australia 15 years ago and has now become virtually obsolete. It may still be used in a few municipalities in formal situations but it is no longer the norm and is therefore not shown. There may be other similar cases.

International Forms of Address

It is not intended to cover the format of address for every country in the world. Such an exercise would be pointless because of the number of combinations and permutations. When dealing with a new international person, either in writing or in face-to-face conversation, it is best to seek advice on the form of address preferred. This can usually be done through the person who has proposed the meeting or contact, by speaking to a personal assistant, by contacting the appropriate consulate, or, in the last resort, asking the person on first meeting how they would like to be addressed. This is the very last resort, but it is better to ask than to go through a meeting with the visitor becoming progressively more annoyed by being incorrectly addressed. You can also fall back on "Sir" or "Madam" for a short meeting, but this fails badly when you want to refer to them in the third person!

It could be helpful to know the basics in the composition of names for some countries in our region. However, let me emphasise that there are many variations and advice on each individual case should be sought:

People's Republic of China

Most Chinese names are made up of two words under the official 'Pinyin' spelling system used to romanise the Mandarin names. Names comprise three syllables - for example, Zhou Enlai. The family name comes first. There are no hyphens connecting the words. The personal name is never placed before the family name. Initials are not used as abbreviations and, unlike some overseas Chinese, Western Christian names are very rarely used. Chinese should be addressed as "Mr", "Mrs", "Madam" or "Miss" followed by their family name - for example, Mr Zhou. Titles such as 'Professor' and 'Dr' are also used. The title 'Comrade' should not be used. In writing, the full name should be used.

Overseas Chinese

There is a wide variation in names depending on where the Chinese is resident and which dialect of Chinese is spoken. 'Tan' and 'Chan' are the same name in Hokkien and Cantonese respectively. The 'Pinyin' spelling system is generally not used and three word names are more common - for example, Low Choon Ming. The family name comes first. The form of spoken address should be 'Mr', 'Mrs' or 'Miss', followed by the family name - for example, Mr Low. In correspondence, the three names should be used. The difficulty comes with Western-influenced Chinese who adopt a Western Christian name and turn their name around to make it easier for Westerners. Some options for Low Choon Ming could be:

> Choon-Ming Low
>
> C M Low
>
> Peter Low or P C M Low

Chinese from Malaysia may also have a Malay title, 'Datuk' or 'Tun', which should be used in place of 'Mr' etc - for example, Datuk Low Choon Ming should be addressed as Datuk Low.

India

The order of first names and surnames differs greatly between regions and it is impossible to lay down a complete guide. Forms of address also vary between Hindus and Sikhs. The English form of address of 'Mr', 'Mrs' and so on is universally acceptable and should be used. Western-style surnames and Christian names are frequently adopted.

Indonesia

With the wide range of religions and ethic groupings in Indonesia, there is a wide range of names and titles, varying from the overseas Chinese to the Javanese, the Sundanese through to the Hindus of Bali. Many Indonesians have only one name (the best known is probably their first President, Soekarno). As a guide, it is never offensive to use the English 'Mr', 'Mrs' and 'Miss' before the first (or only) name. In correspondence, the full name should be used.

Japan

When written in Japanese, the family name comes first, but when this is translated into English, the order is invariably reversed. If you see the name Mr Hideki (or H) Ogasawara, the person should be addressed as "Mr Ogasawara". When speaking, the suffix 'San' is frequently added to the family name and simply means 'Mr', 'Mrs' or 'Miss' - for example, Ogasawara-san. This style should not be used by English speakers until a relationship has been established, so it is safer to use the more formal English words. Even among friends, the given name is infrequently used as a form of address and should never be used by English speakers. The pronunciation of some Japanese family names can appear daunting. You will give a very acceptable pronunciation if you break the name into two or three-letter groups and pronounce each of them - for example, Ogasawara becomes Oga-sa-wa-ra.

Korea

Korean names follow a similar pattern to the Chinese. The first name in any group of names is the family name. The second name can be written in several ways - for example, Kim Syng Joo or Kim Syng-joo or Kim Syngjoo. The person should be addressed as 'Mr Kim'. In correspondence, the three names should be used. However, like overseas Chinese, Koreans frequently invert their names when dealing with English speakers. If they do this, they frequently (but not always) show the family name in bold on business cards which is a real help.

Malaysia

Malays generally have one or two names. In addition to the given names, the name of the father is added after the word 'bin' (for males) and 'binte' (for females). The name Abdul Rahman bin Ahmad Khan means Abdul Rahman, son of Ahmad Khan. However, there is a growing tendency for the word 'bin' or 'binte' to be dropped and the name to become Rahman Khan. He should be addressed as "Mr Rahman". In correspondence, the full name should be used. Some Western-educated Malays may adopt a Western-given name similar to the overseas Chinese. There are a number of other titles/forms of address used as prefixes. The most common are:

Encik	roughly equivalent to 'Mr'
Cik	roughly equivalent to 'Mrs' or 'Miss'
Tuan	a title of respect for older or distinguished people whom one would address as 'Sir' in English. The female equivalent is 'Puan'.
Syed	this indicates descent from the Prophet and is invariably used in conjunction with Tuan.
Haji	this indicates the person has made the pilgrimage to Mecca. The female equivalent is 'Hajjah'. This title is preceded by 'Tuan' or 'Puan' as appropriate.
Tun	this is the highest honour that can be bestowed on a commoner by the King of Malaysia. The wife of a 'Tun' takes the title 'Toh Puan'.
Tan Sri	this is equivalent to the British honour of a knighthood. The wife takes the title 'Puan Sri'.

Datuk   this is roughly equivalent to a British knighthood but below the status of a 'Tan Sri'. The older spelling of 'Dato' is still sometimes seen. The wife takes the title 'Datin' but females can become a 'Datin' in their own right.

Tunku   this is a royal title roughly equivalent to prince or princess. It is only granted to male and female descendants of sultans. It is sometimes spelled 'Tengku'.

Philippines

Christians follow the general Western style of address. The first name is the given name, the second name (frequently shortened to an initial) is the mother's maiden name or the person's maiden name in the case of a married woman, and the last name is the paternal name or the husband's paternal name in the case of a married woman. Muslims often observe a similar pattern, although the style of names previously described under Indonesia or Malaysia are quite common.

Thailand

Most Thais have two names. The first is the given name and the second is the family name. The spelling of Thai names in romanised form is very difficult due to the phonetic language and there is no standard system of transliteration. Thais follow an individual style so the romanised form may not be consistent or even strictly phonetic. In conversation, it is correct to apply 'Mr', 'Mrs' or 'Miss' to the given name which is generally shorter and more easily pronounced than the family name. In addressing letters, the full name should be used, but the salutation should use the given name - for example, the envelope would be addressed to Mr Sataya Nicrothanonda with the salutation being "Dear Mr Sataya". There are many titles, including royal titles, used in Thailand. Where these are known, they should be used with the given name.

Vietnam

Most Vietnamese have three names such as Tran Thi Ngan or Nguyen Dang Nghia. The first name is the family name. Many refer to one of the old royal dynasties - for example, Nguyen (now challenging Smith as the most prominent name in Australian telephone directories), Tran, Le, Ly, Ho and so on. The middle name may indicate gender or, combined with the third name, may have some poetic meaning. 'Van' is the most common middle name for males, while 'Thi' is common for females. The last name is the given name by which people are addressed - for example, "Mr Nghia" but never "Mr Dang Nghia". In correspondence, the full name should be used. Some Vietnamese, especially women, have four names, with the last two generally hyphenated. These last two names generally have a poetic meaning and should be used together as the given name.

For Further Information

- Contact the appropriate protocol office listed in Appendix A.

* * *

Visits by important dignitaries place pressure on the hosts. Very composed and confident people can become quite nervous waiting for the dignitaries to arrive. The Prince and Princess of Wales were visiting a rural community. One of the duties of the advance protocol officer, who arrived 15 minutes ahead of the main party, was to check that arrangements were in place and to have a calming word to the waiting hosts. "Everything looks fine - nothing to worry about," he said to the waiting Mayoress. "That's good," she replied, "we are all so excited." "Everything is under control but I suppose your husband is a little nervous?", he said. "Oh, no," she replied, " he is quite calm. He is a smoke-piper."

TITLES

Titles are not widely used in Australia. We are an egalitarian society. With the cessation of the awarding of knighthoods under the Imperial system of honours and awards in 1992, the number of persons entitled to use the title 'Sir' or 'Dame' is slowly declining.

There are the everyday titles in common use such as 'Doctor', 'Professor' and 'Councillor'. These are well understood and are not covered in this book. The ones that do cause some confusion are discussed below.

His/Her Excellency

In Australia, this title is only used by the Governor-General, the spouse of the Governor-General, the State Governors and Ambassadors/High Commissioners. Its use has been carried forward from the 19th century.

There have been some personal views on the title expressed by some Vice-Regal office-holders in recent years. This has related to being addressed face to face and in the salutation of correspondence as "Your Excellency". Some have a preference to be addressed in correspondence either by name - for example, "Dear Sir William" or as "Dear Governor". In face-to-face conversation, 'Governor' has been preferred. You will never be wrong to use the formal method of address but it is courteous to follow any known preference. If you are going to host the Governor-General or a Governor at a function, a staff member will offer advice during the reconnaissance visit.

In the Northern Territory and the external territories, the Administrator uses the title 'His/Her Honour' rather than 'His/Her Excellency'.

With the diplomatic corps the title is part of the international diplomatic code of practice. This also varies with some countries where the title 'Ambassador' is preferred to 'Your Excellency'. As before, the formal method of address is never wrong but be guided by known preferences.

The Right Honourable

The use of this title flows from the United Kingdom where membership of the Privy Council entitles members to be designated 'The Right Honourable'. The Privy Council is a body which used to be the source of all executive power in the United Kingdom but is now an advisory body to the Sovereign. All British Cabinet Ministers are members and some Australian high office-holders were invited to join.

Membership was given sparingly and included Governors-General, Prime Ministers, some senior Commonwealth Ministers, Leaders of the Opposition and some High Court Justices. Not all holders of these offices accepted the invitation to join. No State parliamentarians or justices have been appointed to the Privy Council for more than 100 years.

The passing of the *Australia Act* in 1986 removed the right of Australians to appeal to the Privy Council in legal matters. No Australians have been appointed to the Privy Council since that time and it appears unlikely that any Australians will be appointed in future. With the passage of time, the title will slip into disuse in Australia.

There is often confusion with the title used by the Lord Mayors of Australian capital cities (other than Darwin). The title 'The Right Honourable' is part of the title of the office and does not involve membership of the Privy Council. As an example, the full title for former Prime Minister Malcolm Fraser, who is a member of the Privy Council, is:

> The Right Honourable Malcolm Fraser, AC, CH
> former Prime Minister of Australia

The title for a Lord Mayor (other than the Lord Mayor of Darwin) is:

> Councillor Peter Murdoch
> The Right Honourable the Lord Mayor of Melbourne

The Honourable

The title 'Honourable' is quite widely used throughout Australia. The authority for this title goes back originally to approvals granted from the United Kingdom in colonial times. It has now been accepted in Australia through long use and established practice. This title applies to the following office holders:

- Commonwealth and State Ministers of the Crown (but not Ministers in the Australian Capital Territory Government).
- Commonwealth parliamentary secretaries
- Presiding officers of the State lower Houses of Parliament.
- All members of the State upper Houses of Parliament (does not apply to Queensland and the Northern Territory which are unicameral parliaments).
- Justices of the Australian High Court, the Federal Court, the Family Court, and all State Supreme Courts.

After retirement from office, Ministers of the Commonwealth, Victoria and Tasmania automatically retain the title for life. Commonwealth parliamentary secretaries automatically retain the title for life.

Ministers of other governments apply to the Governor of the State concerned to retain the title.

All other office-holders may apply to the Governor-General or appropriate Governor to retain the title. There is usually some time qualification in the office before approval can be granted. However, approval is procedural and, if the time constraints have been met, it is invariably granted. The one exception to this rule is that justices in the Northern Territory retain the title automatically.

Municipalities

There has been a major reorganisation of local government in most States over the past decade with some simplification in the range of titles of elected representatives.

The title 'Councillor' is now used by all elected local government representatives in Victoria, Queensland, South Australia, Tasmania and the Australian Capital Territory. The other States have a mixture of Aldermen and Councillors. In Western Australia, where some municipalities have two elections, one for the council and one for the mayor, it is possible that the Mayor will not be a member of council and will have no special title!

The names of municipalities are also very varied. There are cities, towns, shires, regional councils and district councils. The leaders may be known as mayors, shire presidents or chairs.

Local government organisation is still settling down and no effort will be made to cover all the possibilities. It is best to contact the local government association in your area for detailed advice.

The Title 'Royal'

There are many organisations in Australia that bear the title 'Royal'. Some are national in character, such as the Royal Australasian College of Surgeons, and others are more local, such as the Royal Melbourne Yacht Club. The granting of the title brings no specific benefit to the organisation concerned other than some social recognition. It does not indicate that the organisation has any special rights, excellence or competence over similar bodies that do not have the title.

The title 'Royal' is personally granted to an organisation by the Sovereign, but the practice has largely fallen into disuse. There have been no approvals given in the past decade and there are very few applications. The rules governing approval have changed over the years. Many titles were granted in the 1920s and 1930s when the rules were quite different to today. To be considered now, an organisation must meet the following guidelines:

- Be devoted to national, charitable or scientific objects.
- Be of eminence, long-standing and with a secure financial position.

Universities, schools and colleges, hospitals (other than the transfer of a title to an amalgamated or substituted hospital), sporting clubs, theatres or any commercial application will no longer be considered.

Application is made, in the first place, through the appropriate Premier for State-based organisations and through the Prime Minister for national bodies. In 1994, Prime Minister Keating said he would not process any further requests. Prime Minister Howard has not yet been tested.

For Further Information

- Contact the appropriate protocol office listed in Appendix A.

- See Appendix E for some details on methods of address.
- Contact the local government association in your capital city for details of the municipal organisation and methods of address. The telephone numbers are in the capital city White Pages.

* * *

A verger at an Anglican cathedral became a little strange. He left the established church and started his own, which he operated out of his garage at home. He attracted a dozen or so followers and conducted services there. He declared himself the Bishop of his church and obtained some very impressive, highly coloured robes, including a mitre considerably larger than that of the Anglican Archbishop. He insisted that he be addressed as 'Your Grace' and that his followers kiss his hand. After a few months, he decided to show that his church should be taken seriously by attending a major ecumenical function at the Anglican cathedral wearing full regalia. As he approached the entrance, he was spotted by an Anglican minister who had known him in his previous life. The minister greeted him with "G'day Rod, what's with the gear?" He turned on his heel and was never seen again.

TABLES OF PRECEDENCE

A table of precedence is used to determine the ranking of holders of high office attending a function or ceremony. It gives guidance for the order of introductions, seating or positions in a procession.

Who Has a Table of Precedence

There are two general tables of precedence which most organisations use for guidance:

- Commonwealth Table of Precedence This sets out the relative importance of certain office holders in the eyes of the Commonwealth Government. It covers Australia as a whole and recognises office-holders at the Commonwealth and State levels.

- State Tables of Precedence All States other than Western Australia have a separate table of precedence. In Western Australia, they generally follow the pattern of other States. These tables show the relative importance of certain office holders in the eyes of the respective State governments.

There is no reason why any organisation cannot establish its own table of precedence. Any organisation may determine a ranking of office holders as it sees them. The difficulty is that any such table will only have very limited recognition and if it varies greatly from the standard Commonwealth or State table it is likely to create more confusion than order. Most people use one of the standard tables and apply the practice of 'honorary precedence' which is described later.

There are two tables - which one do I use? Any function hosted by the Commonwealth Government or one of its agencies applies the Commonwealth table, irrespective of where the function is located. State governments or agencies use the appropriate State table.

Which table should the Shire of Lower Gordon use for the ceremony to open a new children's playground it has constructed in the municipality? The State Minister for Local Government is the guest of honour who has been invited to open the facility and the State Government provided a $150,000 grant toward the project. In this case there is little doubt that the State table would be used.

Not so clear is the opening of a road bridge which will be jointly performed by the responsible Commonwealth and State Ministers, as both governments provided funding to the project. Clearly, one name has to appear before the other on the commemorative plaque and one has to be introduced and speak before the other. The Mayor can only accompany one of the ministers in any ceremonial procession. Both governments are important to the municipality and the Mayor does not wish to offend either. This is where the skills of the organising or protocol officer are required. I will leave you to ponder your solution.

How do you Use a Table of Precedence

Like most things in protocol, the tables of precedence should be used as guidelines rather than strict inviolable rules. The application of the table to the particular situation must make sense and must not appear contrived. The tables are designed to help make a function flow smoothly, not to create difficulties for either the hosts or the guests. The tables are not frequently changed, which indicates that they are more in the nature of guidelines. The Commonwealth table has not changed since 1982.

All office-holders mentioned in the tables know where they fall in seniority and are also aware that 'honorary precedences' are invariably applied at almost every function. They are used to minor variations but they must not be extreme.

What are Honorary Precedences?

Not all office-holders are listed in the tables of precedence. To attempt to do so would result in unworkable documents. For example, university chancellors and vice-chancellors are not mentioned. Neither are mayors and other elected municipal officers. However, they are frequently key players in ceremonies who need to be interleaved into the standard tables, depending on the occasion.

A function relating to the opening of a tertiary education facility could see university chancellors or vice-chancellors playing a key role, whereas the municipal leader may be of comparatively minor consideration. The relative importance of the university leaders to **this** function should be recognised by interleaving them into the table of precedence at a comparatively high level. This is known as an 'honorary precedence' which only applies to **this** function.

There are also instances of the application of 'honorary precedences' to office-holders already named in the tables of precedence. The tables of precedence set a level for Ambassadors and High Commissioners. The Prime Minister of Japan is visiting and an official lunch is being held in his honour. A number of Ambassadors have been invited. There is no doubt that the Japanese Ambassador would be accorded a precedence above his colleagues. You would see the Ambassador probably sitting at the main table at lunch. His colleagues would be seated at tables appropriate to their order in the table of precedence in the body of the hall. This is commonsense and would be expected by all present. It looks sensible and natural.

However, persons named on a table of precedence are never given a lower 'honorary precedence'.

What About the Bridge Opening?

There is no definitive solution but you could consider the following:

- The Mayor meets both Ministers on arrival with the Deputy Mayor. The first to arrive waits at the arrival point and then both Ministers with the Mayor and Deputy Mayor walk to the dais together.
- The Mayor sits centrally with a Minister on either side.
- After the Mayor welcomes the guests, he invites the Minister sitting on his left (the junior position) to speak first. The other Minister speaks immediately afterwards.
- The cutting of the ribbon (or other ceremonial opening ceremony) is jointly conducted by the Mayor and the two Ministers

- (?three pairs of scissors or one large ceremonial pair of scissors they can all hold).
- The order of names on the plaque is according to some reason (degree of financial or other support) If all else fails, in alphabetical order.
- The draft order-of-arrangements document, including the wording on the plaque, is sent to each Minister's office for information well before the ceremony. The order of arrangements is sent for information, not for approval. This will allow any reaction from either of the offices to be worked through and resolved before the event. The aim is to ensure that there are no surprises, difficulties or embarrassments on the day.

For Further Information

- Contact the appropriate protocol office listed in Appendix A to obtain a copy of the appropriate State Table of Precedence.
- The Commonwealth Table of Precedence is published as the Commonwealth of Australia Gazette S206 of October 5, 1982.

* * *

Melbourne Airport had a VIP aircraft arrival apron. It was a freight terminal by night and a VIP terminal by day. There were four aluminium flag poles along one side which added a little formality to an otherwise rather uninspiring piece of tarmac. During the final reconnaissance on the day before the Prince and Princess of Wales arrived for their first visit, the airport manager noticed that one of the flag poles was slightly bent and instructed his maintenance manager to get it straightened.

The following morning, about three hours before the arrival ceremony, the airport manager telephoned and asked if I would like the good news or the bad news. At this stage of proceedings I opted for the good news.

"You recall the flag pole that was being straightened?", he said, "I think we will have it welded together again before the arrival."

The maintenance manager's solution to straightening the flag pole was to lasso the pole with a piece of rope, which was then attached to the towbar of a truck. The truck tugged a little vigorously and aluminium tubing does not bend very well.

It was fixed in time but it was the most welded and reinforced flag pole in Australia.

STATE FUNERALS

A state funeral is the final recognition of the service of an individual by a government. Both the Commonwealth and State Governments conduct these funerals as 'state funerals'.

State funerals have a long history. They were introduced in the 19th century when Members of Parliament were generally not paid. There were cases where former senior Government Ministers were given paupers' funerals as the families could not afford a more appropriate service. Governments decided that if a Minister's family could not afford a proper service, then the Government should make the arrangements and meet the costs. This practice has continued, and developed, despite all Members of Parliament now being adequately compensated financially for their work.

Although there are some variations among the States on who normally receives a state funeral, they are generally offered to the families of serving and former Governors-General, Governors, Ministers, parliamentary presiding officers and Chief Justices of the senior judicial court. There is no specific entitlement and each case is approved by the Prime Minister or Premier.

State funerals may be offered to the families of any Australian citizen where the Prime Minister or Premier considers their service to Australia or the State to be outstanding and believes that public recognition of that service through a state funeral would be appropriate. Such cases are comparatively rare but have included the distinguished war surgeon Sir Edward (Weary) Dunlop in 1993 and Aboriginal elder and leader Charles Perkins in 2000. All States have agreed to hold a state funeral for the last World War I veteran to pass away in their State.

A state funeral does not differ greatly from a normal family funeral. The format of the service is determined by the family in consultation with the appropriate church minister or funeral celebrant. The specific elements of a state funeral are:

- All costs, other then the headstone, are met by the Commonwealth or State Government. This applies to the service only. The maintenance of the funeral site remains that of the family. The cost of any wake or gathering after the service remains the responsibility of the family.
- Official death and funeral notices are inserted in the appropriate daily newspapers in addition to any personal notices inserted by the family.
- The Australian National Anthem is played at an appropriate stage of the service - normally at the beginning.
- The Australian National Flag is draped over the coffin or casket with the canton (the corner of the Australian Flag containing the Union Flag) over the deceased's heart.
- Official mourners are seated on one side of the church or hall with the family mourners and friends being seated on the other.
- There is a formal seating arrangement for the official mourners. This is arranged and supervised by government officers.

- An official wreath is placed at the foot of the coffin or casket. This is normally provided even if the family requests some other form of recognition other than floral tributes.
- An official mourner, such as the Prime Minister or the Premier, may be asked to read a lesson or deliver a tribute, but this is solely a matter for the family to decide.
- There is frequently some ceremonial, such as a police motorcycle escort, to lead the funeral procession from the service to the cemetery or crematorium.

It is not always appropriate to hold a state funeral due to religious requirements or the timing of the death. In these circumstances, a state memorial service will often be held some time after the actual interment or cremation, which has been conducted as a family service. In such cases, the general arrangements applicable to a state funeral will apply although the government normally only meets the cost of the memorial service. State memorial services can also be held when the person dies overseas and a local funeral service is not possible. This was the case with Sir Rohan Delacombe, a former Governor of Victoria for 11 years, who died in England in 1991.

For Further Information

- Contact the appropriate protocol office listed in Appendix A.

* * *

A former Minister of Health in the Victorian Government lived on a dairy property near Corryong bordering the Murray River. It was real 'Man from Snowy River' country. He arranged that he could be buried on his property and, when the time came, a state funeral service was conducted in a church in Corryong and the casket was then transported to the property. He had been a prisoner-of-war in Changi and the family asked that a military bugler play at the burial.

It was late in the afternoon when the casket was placed on the back of a Land Rover to carry it up the hill to the grave site. The cows were making their leisurely way towards the milking shed. The sun was setting on this beautiful valley and casting long shadows that highlight the Australian bushland in that very special way. As the casket was lowered into the grave, the bugler sounded the poignant notes of the Last Post which echoed around the valley. The cows immediately started a melancholy lowing.

An unforgettable experience, which is unlikely to be repeated.

Chapter 4

Honours and Awards

The Australian system of honours and awards was introduced by the Whitlam Government in 1975. The aim was to replace the Imperial system of honours and awards that had been used in Australia since Federation. Awards in the Imperial system were still used by some States and the Commonwealth (generally when under Coalition Governments) until 1992 when all jurisdictions agreed to a proposal from The Queen that only the Australian system should be used. This period of 1975-1992 was a confusing one, with some award nominees wishing to have one of the new Australian awards and others preferring to remain with the established Imperial system. It was also a period of 'double dipping' with a lot of awards being available per head of population.

The initial aim was to replace every award available to Australian citizens under the Imperial system with a comparable one in the Australian system. Since that time there has been an expansion of the

Australian system with new awards becoming available to recognise some specialised service areas. The Australian system is now fully accepted within the community as the only system of honours and awards for Australian citizens. They are no longer referred to as 'Gough's Gongs'.

A few of the Imperial awards have been incorporated into the Australian system as Australian awards. These are awards that are given personally by the Sovereign and are not subject to the recommendation of a government. The most common awards are those given within the Royal Victorian Order for personal service to the Sovereign.

There are two awards in the system where Australian citizens are involved in the nomination process and it is these that will be described in this chapter. These are the Order of Australia and the Australian Bravery Decorations.

The dedicated awards, which are only available to specialised sections of the community and are not subject to community nomination, are not covered. These include such awards as all Australian Defence Force gallantry and conspicuous service awards, the Australian Police Medal, the Emergency Services Medal, the Public Service Medal and the National Medal. Full details of these awards may be found on the website *www.itsanhonour.gov.au*.

Order of Australia

This is the award which is the nation's recognition of meritorious service. It recognises outstanding achievement and contribution. There is no higher honour.

It is not intended to give a detailed history of the Order, although some background is necessary to understand the system today. The aim of this section is to help in the preparation of nominations. The

Order of Australia differs from the Imperial system in a number of ways:

- There is only one 'society of honour' in the Australian system - that is the Order of Australia. The Imperial system had several societies such as the Order of the British Empire (GBE, KBE/DBE, CBE, OBE, MBE and BEM) and the Order of St Michael and St George (GCMG, KCMG/DCMG, CMG).
- There are four levels in the Order of Australia rather than the five or so levels common in the Imperial system. These are Companion (AC), Officer (AO), Member (AM) and Medal (OAM). There was a fifth level of knighthood (AK/AD) introduced during a Coalition Government period of office. There were only nine awards made and this level has been discontinued since 1986.
- Awards are made by the Governor-General on the advice of the Order of Australia Council. This is an independent Council which reports directly to the Governor-General. There is no political involvement. This contrasts with the Imperial system where nominations were made direct to The Queen by the Prime Minister and the Premiers. The 'political patronage' has been removed.
- The only basis for an award is merit. Any person can be awarded any level. There are no restrictions on a person's social standing that disbars them from a particular level such as existed in the Imperial system.

How does the System Work

Anyone can nominate any Australian citizen for an award by completing the nomination form. This form has comprehensive guidelines attached to it to help in its completion. The nomination papers are then forwarded to the honours secretariat in the Governor-General's office. The honours secretariat prepares the nomination for consideration by the Order of Australia Council. This involves contacting the referees that the nominator has suggested and also researching the nomination in some detail. This usually involves contacting a range of independent referees that the secretariat feels may be able to provide additional comment on the meritorious nature of the nomination. The Council meets twice yearly to consider the nominations and passes its recommendations to the Governor-General for approval. Once this has been given, successful nominees are contacted by the Governor-General's office to check that they are agreeable to receiving the award. This is necessary as there may be special circumstances which were not known to the Council where the nominee would prefer not to accept an award at this time, or possibly not at all. There are usually 1-2 per cent of the successful nominations which fall into this category. The successful awards are then published twice yearly in a Commonwealth Government Gazette on Australia Day in January and on the Queen's Birthday holiday in June. They are widely publicised in the news media. The insignia of the awards are presented at investitures held at Government Houses throughout Australia by the Governor-General and the Governors, normally in April/May and September/October following the formal announcement.

Awards are not made posthumously. However, Council will consider all nominations submitted even though the nominee may have passed away after the nomination has been submitted and before it is formally considered by Council. Similarly, any successful nominee who passes away before the formal announcement of the award still receives the award. It is post-dated to the date the nomination was received by the honours secretariat. The rationale is that if the Council had convened that day and had available to it comprehensive nomination material, an award would have been made before death.

What makes a Good Nomination

The first requirement for a good nomination is to have a good nominee. No degree of flashy presentation and slick wording will help if the basic meritorious service is not evident. The Council members have seen too many of these over the years. However, a clear and logical presentation with the key elements highlighted can make the consideration easier for the Council members.

The detail on the printed nomination form generally asks for administrative detail and is easy to complete. Make sure all questions are answered.

The accompanying statement or citation by the nominator is very important as this tells the Council why you think the person should receive an award. The one page provided on the nomination form is rarely sufficient. One or two typewritten pages are normally required. The following comments may help your thought processes:

- The only basis for an award is **merit**. The person must have done something special that makes them stand out from the pack. This may be demonstrated achievement at a high level; it may be a contribution over and above what might be reasonably expected through paid employment or it may be a voluntary contribution to the community which stands out from others who may have made a similar valuable contribution.

- Within an established organisation there will always be a chairperson or president. It is important to show how the nominee's contribution has been more meritorious than that of their predecessors. What have they done that is more special? We are all aware of some presidents who keep the chair warm for possibly a long period of time but do not really advance the aims of the organisation.

- The degree and value of the contribution is far more important that the length of service. Awards in the Order of Australia are not long-service awards. Where a person has held an office for a long time, there is often no comparison with others on the quality of the service. We are all aware of some fairly moribund organisations in which the committee has not changed for years. This is not to say that long service does not show a commitment to the organisation, but it is only one element and not the most important.

- Membership of organisations is not normally the basis for an award. Nominations are received which contain lists of dozens of organisations to which the nominee has belonged. For example, it starts with the Guides when she is 10 years' old, moves through a variety of community organisations, and concludes as a long-time member of the hospital auxiliary now she is 60 years' old. However, there is no detail of what was done in any of them. Did she hold any responsible office? What was achieved in that office? We are all aware that the community has 'joiners' and 'doers'.

- Some people are 'self-starters'. They have an idea to set up an organisation or provide a service to the community where none exists. They form a committee and usually face a daunting task in driving through their idea to a successful conclusion with problems of gaining community support, finding finance and battling the minefield of bureaucratic regulation. If this is the case the pioneering aspect of the contribution should be highlighted. This generally requires a greater contribution than taking over as president in an established organisation for a one-year term.

- We are all aware of many people surmounting overwhelming personal problems in their lives. Overcoming personal tragedies or special service within a family environment, meritorious as that undoubtedly is, may not be as highly regarded as providing a service to the wider community. If both circumstances exist, a very strong case can be made.

- Australian society would collapse without voluntary community service. There would be very few people who do not give some degree of voluntary help to a community ideal. The nomination must show how that service goes above and beyond that which could reasonably be expected of others in a similar position.

- Some nominations concentrate on the nominee's financial contribution to the success of a project, perhaps in the hope that an award will lead to a further contribution. Has that person made any personal physical contribution to the project? Has the funding come from a commercial organisation, of which the nominee is managing director, where there could be some public relations benefit for the firm concerned? What is the value of a $100,000 contribution to a multi-millionaire compared to a $200 contribution from an old-age pensioner?

What About Referees?

Statements from referees are not required to accompany the nomination, but the names and addresses of people who could provide a meaningful comment on the service performed are required. The honours secretariat will contact them independently, as well as others who may be able to offer a comment. The nomination guidelines suggest about five people should be nominated but it can be more. The following comments may help in selecting good referees:

- Ideal referees are people who personally know of the service and can comment from direct personal experience.

- Persons who are intimately involved are not always the best referees. For example, a nomination for the president of an organisation with the referees named being the secretary, the treasurer, the immediate past president and two committee members would not be very helpful to the Council. It could be regarded as too 'in-house'.

- Referees who are regarded as high profile in the community are frequently named as referees in the belief that these names will assist the nomination. Members of Parliament and mayors are regularly nominated but they frequently only have a very general idea of what has been done. Their support letters start with "I have been told..." or "After checking with council staff I understand...." This is second and third-hand information and is not particularly useful. The nominated referees should have first-hand information.

- Referees should support the statements made in the nominator's citation or summary of service. If it is claimed that the nominee has a national or international profile with their work, then there should be some referees from interstate or overseas around the same level as the nominee who can confirm this and comment on the value of the service.

- Some of the best referees are those who are involved in the same type of work but come from different organisations. If the leader of an Anglican welfare organisation was being nominated for the outstanding work she has done with homeless youth, it would be helpful to know how the Uniting Church welfare organisation, as well as St Vincent de Paul and the Salvation Army in the same area, consider she has performed. If they are not included in the nominee's referee list, they are likely to be approached by the honours secretariat when they carry out their independent research.

What Should I do as a Referee?

You may be approached by the Honours Secretariat to provide referee comment. Here are some guidelines that may help:

- Avoid letters that are flowery but say nothing. They are not helpful to Council's consideration of the nomination. Compare the following examples:

Tom has given outstanding service to this community. His dedicated involvement has extended over many years. He has given freely of his time and the community is indebted to his magnificent community spirit. He has been a leader in more projects than I can name and I will leave it to others to describe them in detail. He is particularly well-known for his recent work in the development of the Margaret Creek Skateboard Park. Throughout the community he is known as 'Mr Fix-it of Margaret Creek'. He is an inspiration to all. As the local Member of Parliament for the past 14 years, I have no hesitation in giving this nomination my strongest support. He is the most community-minded citizen I have ever met.

* * *

I am president of the Youth Affairs Council in Margaret Creek. Tom was concerned that the youth of the community had nowhere safe to ride their skateboards where they had some degree of supervision. He had approached the local council with a proposal and, although getting an agreement in principle, nothing had happened for two years. Tom decided to get some action. He formed a citizen's committee comprising members of the local service clubs, the retailers association and community leaders. Tom was the chairman and driving force throughout this project. In the space of six months he has:

- *raised $35,000 from the community through raffles and doorknock appeals.*

- *submitted a proposal to the Minister of Sport for a grant of funds. He received the Minister's full support and a promise of a $50,000 grant on condition that it was matched by a similar grant from the local council.*
- *he submitted a proposal to council for the park suggesting three possible locations. One was selected and Tom then visited all neighbouring residents personally and overcame their objections to the proposal. This was a massive effort involving all his free time, day and night, for some weeks.*
- *council agreed to the additional funding and also agreed to donate the site. However, there was still a funding shortfall. Tom arranged with the local earthmoving contractor to supply his services free of charge to prepare the site and then organised community working bees to further develop the area. Tom was personally present to encourage and guide every such activity.*
- *the new skateboard park was opened jointly late last year by the Minister for Sport and the Mayor. Without Tom's countless hours of determined work and community leadership, the project would not have got off the ground. This is one of many community projects that has Tom's thumbprint on it.*

Which letter was the most helpful to you in assessing Tom's commitment?

- Letters do not need to be long but should tell the facts as you see them without too many superlatives. No more than one page is necessary.
- Avoid one-line replies such as: "I would prefer not to comment on this nomination." This leaves the Council wondering whether you know that the nominee has a criminal record, is suspected of anti-social behaviour or that you had a personal falling-out five years ago. If you do not wish to comment, give

Other Bravery Awards

There are also two private societies operating in Australia whose aim is to recognise brave conduct. These are the Royal Humane Society of Australasia and the Royal Humane Society of New South Wales. There is an historic reason why there are two. However, the latter caters for New South Wales residents and the former looks after all other areas of Australia. Their awards are highly regarded but they are private organisations and their awards do not represent the nation's recognition of brave conduct. The basic requirements of both systems are the same, except that the humane societies have an element of 'risking life to save life'. The 'saving life' element is not a requirement to be awarded an Australian Bravery Decoration.

Post-Nominals

Post-nominals apply to many of the awards in the Australian system of honours and awards. These are a group of letters that appear after the recipient's name to show that they have been recognised by their country for outstanding service or bravery. Some examples have already been given. Others are the Australian Fire Service Medal (AFSM), Public Service Medal (PSM) and the Conspicuous Service Cross (CSC)

The regulations say that they may be used "where the use of post-nominals is customary" and then give no examples of what 'customary' means. Here are some guidelines:

- In addresses on envelopes and on business letters.
- Where lists of names are shown - for example, a list of directors/patrons that may appear on a letterhead.
- On business cards.

- Some people place them after their names in signature blocks, although there would be some argument about whether this is appropriate.
- They would not normally be used in the text of a document unless it was very formal and there was already some precedent.

There can be some confusion with post-nominals that have a specific meaning in a particular profession. A number of State governments have recently changed the title of Queen's Counsel (QC) to Senior Counsel (SC). The letters QC were shown after the name of these senior barristers. The post-nominal has now been replaced with SC. This could indicate that there are many people in the legal profession who have been awarded the Star of Courage. It is unlikely to cause a major problem, but a junior suburban lawyer awarded a Star of Courage may need to explain the circumstances to some senior members of the legal profession!

Precedence of Awards

Where people have received a number of awards, there needs to be an order in which they are worn and in which any post-nominals are listed. This order is established in a Commonwealth Government Gazette entitled *The Order of Wearing Australian Honours and Awards*. As new awards are introduced, the gazette is amended. The current publication is available from Commonwealth Government bookshops listed in Appendix G; it is also shown on the honours website at *www.itsanhonour.gov.au*. This information is particularly relevant to ex-servicemen and women or uniformed services where they may also have war service or long service medals to be worn.

The Gazette shows the relative order of both Australian and Imperial awards as a consolidated list. This is important as there are many members of the community who received Imperial awards before the Australian awards were introduced.

A person was made a Member of the British Empire (MBE) in 1972 for services to the rural industry and was subsequently made a Member of the Order of Australia (AM) for service to the wine industry in 1988. In 1999, he received an Australian Fire Service Medal (AFSM) for service to the rural fire brigade organisation. In what order are they shown? The honours table of precedence has the answers. *(To save you looking it up the answer is AM, MBE, AFSM.)*

Wearing of Awards

There is a detailed booklet on the wearing of awards available from the honours secretariat. It is called *A Guide to the Wearing of Insignia*. However, there is some general confusion over what insignia should be worn and on what occasion. Without getting into the great detail listed in the booklet, the following may be helpful:

- If you have more than one medal you should get them (both the full-sized and the miniature insignia) properly mounted by a professional medallist. There are a number of medallists in each capital city - consult the Yellow Pages under 'Medals'. Don't worry about the order of mounting - the medallist, if they are worth their salt, will have that information.
- The full insignia is normally worn on a lounge suit or jacket on ex-service occasions such as Anzac Day and Remembrance Day, or at special functions such as state funerals. There may be functions where the host will specify that decorations should be worn at a lounge-suit occasion but these would be comparatively rare. Some ex-servicemen and women with many awards and service medals sometimes wear their miniatures as the weight of the full-sized medals distort their clothing. This is not strictly correct but is a practical response to the problem.
- The miniature insignia is worn to evening functions when dinner jacket (Black Tie) with decorations or, now very infrequently in Australia, evening dress (White Tie) is specified. If

you attend such a function wearing a dark lounge suit, it is still appropriate to wear your miniature insignia.

- Some Australian awards have a lapel badge/brooch as part of the insignia. These include the Order of Australia and the Australian Bravery Decorations. Recipients are encouraged to wear it on their civilian clothing at all times. However, it is not worn if you are wearing either the full-sized or miniature insignia.
- Members of the Australian Defence Force and other uniformed or ceremonial organisations should follow the procedures and customs established by those organisations.

Order of St. John

There has been some confusion regarding membership and awards within the Order of St John. There are two Orders operating in Australia which conduct hospital and first-aid services and both have a long history stretching back several hundred years. They recognise each other and are recognised internationally. The two orders are:

- The Sovereign Military and Hospitaller Order of St John of Jerusalem, called of Rhodes, called of Malta This is generally known as the Sovereign Military Order of Malta (SMOM) and is based on the Roman Catholic tradition. It was formed in the 11th century and the headquarters of the Order is in Rome. Awards of knighthoods and lesser levels of recognition are made by the Order to deserving members. These awards are only used or shown within the Order and are not used in general business or social circles.
- The Grand Priory in the British Realm of The Most Venerable Order of the Hospital of St John of Jerusalem This is normally known as the Most Venerable Order of St. John. It is basically a Protestant breakaway group from the SMOM. The current

body was revived in the 19th century and The Queen is the head of the Order. Awards of knighthoods and lesser levels of recognition are made with similar rules of recognition to the SMOM. This is probably the best-known group in Australia as it provides the first-aid officers at major sporting and community events. As The Queen is head of the Order, awards are given a place in the table of precedence for wearing awards (all levels of award have the same precedence).

A number of bodies using the general name of the Order of St John, but with slight variations to the words in the long titles, have been formed in the United States. There are more than 30 of them. They are generally known as the 'Shickshinny Orders', named after the town in Pennsylvania where they were originally headquartered. One or two operate in Australia. They offer awards from knighthoods down, for which you are asked to pay a quite hefty price. The insignia is very decorative and the higher awards come with cloaks and ornate headwear. Many well-known people have accepted the offer of awards thinking they were being honoured by one of the recognised Orders of St John, only to be sadly disillusioned after they had parted with their money. If you are offered an award for which you have to pay money, you may wish to investigate a little further before accepting the offer.

Replacing Lost Medals

Lost decorations and medals, both Australian and Imperial awards, can be replaced. The replacements are not free. Some insignia is quite expensive so it is probably advisable to have appropriate insurance as most losses are through theft rather than misplacement.

Insignia can also be replaced on the request of the next-of-kin of a deceased recipient but this will only be done once.

The procedures differ slightly for different awards and it is probably best to contact the honours secretariat in the first place for further advice.

For Further Information

- Contact the appropriate protocol office listed in Appendix A.
- Consult the website *www.itsanhonour.gov.au*
- For a nomination form for the Order of Australia or further information in a language other than English, call the honours secretariat's 24-hour toll-free number 1800 552 275.
- For further advice on the honours system or guidance in completing a nomination form, telephone the honours secretariat on (02) 6283 3533.
- Consult the Commonwealth Government Gazette entitled *The Order of Wearing Australian Honours and Awards*.
- For contact with the appropriate Royal Humane Society, consult your local capital city White Pages telephone directory.

* * *

Honours post-nominals can be used to represent other rather more derogatory phrases. The post-nominal OBE was known as Other Buggers' Efforts. However, the best probably related to the Order of St Michael and St George in which the various levels were described as:

CMG	Call Me God
KCMG	Kindly Call Me God
GCMG	God Calls Me God

Chapter 5

Symbols

NATIONAL SYMBOLS

Symbols play an important part in our lives. They are everywhere. Corporations spend a lot of money to promote their commercial symbols to establish their identity in our subconscious mind. They can be graphic and visual, they can be a collection of words or they can be a tune or song.

Australia as a Commonwealth and all the States have a range of identifying symbols, not used in the commercial sense of business corporations, but rather to engender a feeling of identity, pride or national belonging. Following an Olympic or Commonwealth Games, there would be few who have not been reminded of the strong ability of our National Anthem and Flag to bind the nation together in a sense of pride and achievement.

The Australian symbols are the coat of arms, the flag, the anthem, the floral emblem, the colours and the gemstone. There is no official faunal emblem although there is little doubt that the kangaroo would be the universal choice.

The Australian States have a variety of symbols. All have a coat of arms, a flag, a badge, and a floral emblem. Most have a faunal emblem (some have several, including a bird, an animal and a fish) and some have a gemstone or fossil emblem as well. These are the official emblems that have been gazetted by the appropriate governments. They have generally been selected on the basis of the dominance of the animal or object in the State concerned, although Queensland clearly does not have exclusive ownership of the koala nor New South Wales the platypus.

There are also some unofficial symbols associated with particular States. The Australian Scottish associations have been active in promoting specific State tartans so that competitors at national Scottish dancing competitions can wear distinctive tartans. Some States have adopted a design. There are also the colours of uniforms worn by representative State cricket or football teams. These are not always the official colours of the State concerned but have wide recognition and acceptance.

The table at Appendix F shows the details of the official symbols used by the Commonwealth and the States.

The Commonwealth has produced an excellent booklet entitled *Australian Symbols* which sets out the history and meaning of all the Commonwealth and State symbols complete with colour pictures. It is available from Commonwealth bookshops trading as Ausinfo. Contact details in each State are shown in Appendix G.

Use of the National Symbols

Not all national symbols are available for general use. Some, such as the National Anthem, are clearly in the public domain and may be freely used without further permission.

However, most of the others have some restrictions which are covered by Commonwealth and State legislation. This particularly applies to the coats of arms and the State badges where the unauthorised use could imply some Government support or endorsement. The coats of arms and badges belong to the government of the day. They could be regarded as the trade mark of the governments concerned. They relate to the Government and cannot be used by the general community without written permission. They cannot be used for merely showing a Victorian or West Australian affiliation.

Approval will normally be given for a coat of arms to be reproduced for educational purposes but written approval from the appropriate Commonwealth or State body is still required.

For Further Information and Approval to Use any National Symbols

- For further detailed information obtain a copy of *Australian Symbols* through an Ausinfo shop listed in Appendix G.
- For further advice and approval to use Commonwealth symbols, contact:

    Awards and National Symbols Branch
    Department of the Prime Minister and Cabinet
    3-5 National Circuit
    BARTON ACT 2600
    Telephone: (02) 6271 5601 Facsimile: (02) 6271 5662

- For further advice and approval to use State symbols contact the appropriate protocol office shown in Appendix A.

* * *

The Queen was leaving Victoria on the Royal Yacht Britannia to sail to South Australia on a balmy March evening. Station Pier was quite crowded with people who had gathered to see the vessel sail. At the front of the crowd was a large gentleman, about 35 years old, with a well-developed stomach, unshaven and with badly cut hair. He was also wearing a pair of just-fitting jeans and a blue singlet. He was walking up and down and frequently looking towards the direction that the motorcade would arrive. His dress tended to stand out from the rest of the crowd and a couple of plain clothes police officers moved near to him. The Queen arrived to some cheering and clapping but this fellow did not join in and appeared to become more animated. As the Queen reached the deck of Britannia he turned to the crowd and bellowed "Now!" In an exceptionally powerful and rich baritone voice he led the singing of God Save The Queen.

As always, looks can be deceiving.

FLAGS

Flags are used to show an affiliation, a loyalty and a pride in a country, a state, an organisation or an ideal.

It is not intended to cover the many special rules for the flying of flags which apply to maritime and military organisations. The comments here apply to the general display of flags on land by the general community.

Flags fall into a number of general categories. In Australia, these could be described as:

- <u>International Flags</u> These are flags of independent nations recognised by the United Nations.

- Official flags The Aboriginal Flag and the Torres Strait Islander flag were proclaimed as official Australian flags in 1995.
- State Flags These are the flags of the States and Territories of Australia.
- Personal Flags These include the personal flags used by the Governor-General and the State Governors. There are also personal flags used by visiting Heads of State and some commanders of the Australian Defence Force.
- Organisation or House Flags These would include business and community group flags - for example, municipalities, McDonald's, BHP, Scouts, Returned and Services League and the International Olympic Committee.

There are other flags which may not fit neatly into any of the above categories, but there are generally special rules which apply within the organisation which uses them.

Flying of Flags

It is not intended to repeat the rules for flying the Australian and other flags or to give a history of the Australian flag in this book. All the details on the many ways that flags can be displayed, with colour diagrams, are contained in the booklet *Australian Flags*. It is available from Commonwealth bookshops. Contact details in each State are shown in Appendix G.

There is some confusion over the flying of other flags with the Australian flag which are not covered in the booklet. There are also a number of frequently asked questions on the use of flags. Some guidelines are mentioned here:

- International flags take precedence over all other flags. The flag of the host country should always occupy the senior position.

In Australia, the Australian flag should never be flown in an inferior position to any other flag.

- When the Australian flag is flown with other international flags, it is flown in the senior position with the flags of the other international nations displayed in alphabetical order. The size or influence of the country does not set its seniority (what a subjective judgement that could be). The names of the countries are those recognised by the United Nations, so the United Kingdom (not Britain) and the United States of America (not America) come towards the end of the display list.

- Personal flags are only flown while that person is present at the venue or location. The exception here is that the Governor-General's and Governors' personal flags are flown at Government House even though they may be away from the actual residence on other duties during the day. In the case of overnight visits within the State, some lower the Governor's personal flag - others consider that the Governor is still in residence while anywhere in the State. All States lower the personal flag when the Governor leaves the State. The Administrator of the Northern Territory does not have a personal flag.

- Not all international flags are of the same proportions. Australian flags (and most of those of Commonwealth countries) are in the proportion 2:1. The American flag is 19:10. The proportions of the Japanese flag and many European countries flags are 3:2. When they are displayed with the Australian flag, it is important to have a comparable area of flag displayed. The standard size of the Australian flag is 1.8 metres x .9 metres, giving a displayed area of 1.62 square metres. When flown with the Japanese flag you would seek a flag of a size which approximated this displayed area. The International Olympic Committee has a special rule to overcome this problem of equality. By agreement with all competing countries the national flags used at the Sydney Olympic Games in 2000 were made in the proportion of 5:3.

- The size of the flag displayed should match the size of the flag pole. This means that people should not be able to jump up to touch the flag when it is hanging limply on the flag pole. The general height of a flag pole to carry a standard-sized 1.8 metre x .9 metre Australian flag should be around 6 metres. With larger flag poles, the size of the flag should increase so that the display looks sensible and attractive. The Australian flag can be made in any size, but flag manufacturers generally stock the sizes of 1.8 metres x .9 metres, 2.7 metres x 1.35 metres and 3.6 metres x 1.8 metres. There are also smaller sizes generally for use on boats.

- Foreign flags should not be displayed other than with the Australian flag. A question is often asked about flying foreign flags on national days or the visit to an establishment by an important overseas visitor. The appropriate flag can be flown on a second flag pole with the Australian flag being flown on the senior flag pole. Where there is only one flag pole, the Australian and foreign flag can be displayed in the foyer of the building using an internal flag display stand. The only establishments permitted to fly a single foreign flag are diplomatic and consular premises.

- Two flags should never be flown from the same flag pole. McDonald's Restaurants are regular offenders in this regard.

- The Australian flag should not be used to cover a plaque or monument at an unveiling ceremony. Flags are for flying free with all symbolic parts on display.

- The Australian flag should not be used to cover a table or seat or to mask the space between the floor and a table, dais or platform. This also applies to what may be described as 'bunting' - displaying the image of the Australian flag.

- Flags should only be flown when their identity can be determined. This means that if they are flown at night, they should be illuminated. This does not require that they be spotlighted. If the ambient light in the area is sufficient for the flag to be identified, that is satisfactory.

Half-Masting of Flags

Half-masting of flags is a sign of mourning. The half-masting of the Australian flag is authorised by a Commonwealth Government Minister acting for the Prime Minister. There is authority for the Australian flag to be lowered on the death of a distinguished local citizen if approved by the authorities in that city or town. It would only be half-masted in that locality. When an organisation wishes to recognise the passing of a distinguished member of that organisation, it is probably best to fly only the house flag on the day of the funeral in the half-masted position.

The mythology of half-masting is that the normal flag is lowered to allow the invisible flag of death to fly above. The term 'half-masting' is unfortunate as many people think that the flag should be lowered half way down the flag pole. This is not so. The flag should be lowered sufficiently for the 'flag of death', which is theoretically the same size as the lowered flag, to be flown above. However, the lowering of the normal flag needs to be sufficient to avoid giving the impression that the flag has slipped or not been raised properly. In practical terms, lowering about one-third the height of the flag pole is ideal.

A flag is normally only half-masted for one day or part of that day. The day of the funeral is the day usually selected.

The Governor-General's and Governors' personal flags are not lowered as part of a general half-masting. They are only lowered on the death of the Sovereign or a senior member of the Royal Family.

For Further Information

- Contact the appropriate protocol office listed in Appendix A.
- Consult *Australian Flags* available from Ausinfo Bookshops listed in Appendix G.
- For further specialised advice on the Australian Flag, contact:

    Awards and National Symbols Branch
    Department of the Prime Minister and Cabinet
    3-5 National Circuit
    BARTON ACT 2600
    Telephone: (02) 6271 5601 Facsimile: (02) 6271 5662

- For very detailed information on the history and development of all world flags, refer to *The World Encyclopedia of Flags* by Alfred Znamierowski, published by Lorenz Books.
- An informative internet contact is Flags of the World at *www.fotw.digibel.be*

* * *

The Prince and Princess of Wales visited Puckapunyal where Charles, as Colonel-in-Chief of the Royal Australian Armoured Corps, was to present a new guidon to the Corps on a ceremonial parade. As the Prince and Princess were walking from the officers' mess toward the Rolls Royce, which was to take them to the parade ground, I noticed that the Prince's Personal Standard on the small flag pole on the roof of the car was upside down. As they were only five paces from the car, there was nothing to be done other than to hope that nobody noticed. Once the car had uneventfully delivered them to the parade ground, there was a frantic telephone call to the transport officer. At the end of the ceremony, the car returned to the parade ground with the Standard the right way up.

No comments were made. No one had noticed. I wonder why I am admitting this now?

NATIONAL ANTHEMS

National anthems fall into a similar category to national flags. They are an expression of national pride, loyalty and affiliation. They are often used in conjunction with the national flag.

The National Anthem

Australia's National Anthem is the tune known as *Advance Australia Fair*. The authorised words for the two verses of the anthem are shown at Appendix H. This anthem, with the revised words, was adopted in 1984 after a period of some confusion over what the anthem should be and after the original words of *Advance Australia Fair* were widely criticised. Some general guidelines on the use of the National Anthem are:

- Only one verse of the National Anthem is played unless there is choral accompaniment. Even then one verse is the norm. Both verses may be sung if the event is a particularly nationalistic ceremony, such as the flag-raising ceremony on Australia Day, or other special circumstances. If you wish the audience to sing, be aware that very few people know the words to the second verse.
- The National Anthem is only played once at a ceremony. Special arrangements apply for some military ceremonial parades.
- The National Anthem is normally played at the start of an event or as the closing activity.
- It is customary for all who are able to do so to stand and remain silent when the National Anthem is played.
- There is no compulsion for the National Anthem to be played at all events. The choice is up to the organisers of the activity. It should not be played if its inclusion gives the appearance of contrived circumstances. Commonsense will indicate where

participants expect it to be played if a precedent has not been established.

- There is no 'short' version of the National Anthem. (See details on the Vice-Regal Salute below)
- The National Anthem should be played in its authorised form. There should be no variations to 'jazz it up' or otherwise change the standard rendition.

The Royal Anthem

The Royal Anthem is *God Save The Queen*. Australia shared this national anthem with the United Kingdom and many Commonwealth countries before 1984 when we adopted *Advance Australia Fair*. Some guidelines on the use of the Royal Anthem are:

- It is only played as an anthem in the presence of The Queen or a member of the Royal Family.
- The full first verse is only played as an anthem for The Queen, The Duke of Edinburgh and the Queen Mother. Other members of the Royal Family are only entitled to a shortened version comprising the first six and last six bars of the anthem.
- At military ceremonial parades attended by a member of the Royal Family, an anthem is usually played at both the beginning and the end of the parade. The Queen has asked that the Royal Anthem be used for one occasion and the Australian National Anthem be used for the other.
- It is customary for all who are able to do so to stand and remain silent when the Royal Anthem is played.
- At ex-service occasions such as Anzac Day, there is still a wish by some veterans to have *God Save The Queen* played. It is frequently played and sung, not as an anthem, but as a hymn at an appropriate time during the ceremony. The words are contained in the Anglican and Catholic hymn books. It is

normal to sing the first and third verses. The words of the second verse are generally regarded as inappropriate.

- The words of *God Save The Queen* are not as well known in Australia now as in previous years and, if it is to be included as a hymn, the words should be printed in the programme of events.

The Vice-Regal Salute

The Vice-Regal Salute is an abbreviated form of the National Anthem. It is played as a salute to welcome or farewell the Governor-General or a State Governor. It is played as a salute and not as an anthem. It comprises the first four bars and the last four bars of *Advance Australia Fair*. Some guidelines on the use of the Vice-Regal Salute are:

- There are no words for the Vice-Regal Salute. It is a salute to be played, not an anthem to be sung. If the Vice-Regal Salute is to be played, it is wise to advise the audience beforehand that it is not the National Anthem. If some people start to sing, they quickly run out of music! This detracts from the ceremony of the occasion.

- Except on some military occasions the Vice-Regal Salute should only be played once, normally on arrival of the Governor-General or Governor.

- It should not be played when the Governor-General or Governor are walking. It is played once they have reached their position at the dais, podium or table and they and all the accompanying party are motionless.

- It is customary for all who are able to do so to stand and remain silent when the Vice-Regal Salute is played.

Other Anthems

The Australian National Anthem is sometimes played in association with other national anthems, particularly at the start of international sporting events. Unless there is some other established international precedent associated with the event, the Australian National Anthem, as that of the host country, is normally played last.

No more than two national anthems should be played sequentially. Any more and the attention of the audience falls away. If there is pressure for a number of anthems, then only the Australian National Anthem should be played.

For Further Information

- Contact the appropriate protocol office listed in Appendix A.
- Commonwealth Members of Parliament and Senators can provide a cassette containing a military band and a choral version of the Australian National Anthem free of charge. Contact your nearest Commonwealth parliamentary office.
- Consult Commonwealth Gazette S142 of April 19, 1984, as the authority for the Australian National Anthem.

* * *

The Prince and Princess of Wales were performing a major public engagement which was being televised live. The function concluded and the entourage moved on to the next engagement nearby. As the motorcade approached, the host and hostess could not be seen at the agreed meeting point. The Prince and Princess left the car and, professionals that they were, walked over and started speaking to some of the waiting crowd. A few moments later, the embarrassed hosts emerged from the building full of apologies. They had been inside watching the telecast of the previous function. It had been televised with a 20-minute delay.

COATS OF ARMS

Coats of arms originated in the 14th century in the United Kingdom. In simple terms, they were the personal identification badge or design emblazoned on a knight's shield or displayed on a banner so that he and his followers could be identified.

Since that time the rules of heraldry have developed with all matters dealing with coats of arms, for persons and corporations within the Commonwealth, being controlled by the College of Arms in London. The College of Arms acts on authority delegated to it by the Sovereign. It is a very specialised matter and it is not intended to go into any heraldic details in this book. What will be covered is the acquisition and use of coats of arms in Australia, how they can be used and who may use them.

Coats of arms should not be confused with logos or badges. Anyone can produce a logo or badge which may be registered as commercial property. They are normally simple designs which catch the eye to promote a product or an organisation. They can be changed at will. A coat of arms is based on heraldic principles and is registered with the College of Arms. It is a formal symbol which contains elements that are particularly relevant to the holder. They are of long duration: for example, the Australian coat of arms was adopted in 1912 and has not changed in general appearance since that time.

Coats of arms may be granted by the College of Arms to individuals or to corporations.

Personal Coats of Arms: These are granted to an individual who can show that his service to society is something extraordinary. It requires the submission of a personal curriculum vitae, supported by referees, to the College of Arms. If the granting of arms is approved, they may only be used by that particular family. There is no authority for anyone with the same surname to use the coat of arms. We would all be familiar with the commercial exploitation that occurs through sales booths in shopping malls displaying myriad coats of arms where people are exhorted to part with $50 to obtain a plaque displaying their 'family coat of arms'. There is no authority for this and most operators acknowledge this point in the small print of their agreement - but only after you have passed over your money.

<u>Corporate Coats of Arms</u>: These are granted to corporations which can demonstrate that they are committed to giving service to the public. Governments and semi-government bodies are the most obvious examples in Australia. The coats of arms are used to show ownership or visually declare authority. They are used, for example, on Acts of Parliament, seals, buildings, official reports, letterheads and gifts. In all cases they belong to the body to whom they were granted and the general community is not permitted to use them. In the case of State governments, the coat of arms belongs to the government of the day - for example, the Queensland coat of arms belongs to the Government of Queensland. It cannot be used by anyone else to show that they come from Queensland or used on a product to show that it was manufactured in Queensland. All Australian governments have legislation protecting and governing the use of their coats of arms. Use may be permitted for educational and some other purposes, but formal approval is required in each case.

The design and approval of coats of arms costs at least $8000 and may be more expensive depending on the complexity of research and design.

Neither personal nor corporate coats of arms are widely sought in Australia and there has been comparatively little interest in the past decade. Those which have been granted are jealously guarded by their holders.

For Further Information

- Contact the appropriate protocol office listed in Appendix A.
- Consult books on heraldry held by municipal libraries. There are many which give great detail on the heraldic composition of coats of arms.
- Consult an heraldic society in your State. Contact details can be found in the capital city telephone directories.
- At the time of writing, the College of Arms had not completed a web site but the contact address is *www.collegeofarms.co.uk*

* * *

Visitors are frequently asked whether they have any particular likes or dislikes, especially when it comes to food and drink. The response is normally to tell you what is not favoured rather than to give any positive preferences. Before a visit to Australia by Princess Alexandra, there was a well-publicised article in a women's magazine in which she was reported as saying how much she enjoyed strawberries and cream at Wimbledon. The word spread like wildfire. Every dessert at every meal was strawberries and cream.

By the end of the visit she had probably changed her view.

Chapter 6

Other Matters

CONGRATULATORY MESSAGES

There is an Australia-wide system of congratulatory messages for people who reach birthday and wedding anniversary milestones. The system is operated through the Government Houses, the Prime Minister's Department and the Premiers' Departments throughout Australia.

The messages generally take the form of letters which arrive a day or so before the anniversary. The milestones generally recognised - although there are minor differences among the States - are:

60th Wedding Anniversaries (Diamond)

Messages are received from:

- The Queen
- The Governor-General
- The Governor of the State

- The Prime Minister
- The Premier of the State

50th Wedding Anniversaries (Golden)

Messages are received from:

- The Governor of the State
- The Prime Minister
- The Premier of the State

100th Birthdays

Messages are received from:

- The Queen
- The Governor-General
- The Governor of the State
- The Prime Minister
- The Premier of the State

90th Birthdays (not recognised in South Australia)

Messages are received from:

- The Governor
- The Prime Minister
- The Premier of the State

In some States, other individuals and organisations are notified of the anniversary and provide messages. These include Australia Day Councils and Leaders of the Opposition. A message may also be provided by the local Member of Parliament.

Requests for this recognition need to be initiated by family or friends. Congratulatory messages do not happen automatically. To ensure a timely arrival of the messages, four to six weeks' notice should be given.

The offices of all Federal Members of Parliament and most State Members of Parliament, have the necessary nomination forms and know the procedure. You will need to produce a birth or marriage certificate or other similar form of proof when making the application. Statutory declarations will normally be accepted where records have been lost or the only known copy is held by the celebrant and the family wants the messages to be a surprise. If you cannot contact an MP's office, you can contact one of the State protocol offices for further guidance.

For Further Information

- Contact the appropriate protocol office listed in Appendix A.

* * *

A state thanksgiving service was held at a major cathedral for the return of the Navy contingent from the Gulf War. As the guests were arriving for the Sunday morning service, a less-than-well-dressed individual, who was helping himself to refreshment from a bottle in a brown paper bag, was offering them greetings near the church door. He disappeared after the service started and all was proceeding well.

As the Archbishop began his sermon, a familiar and very clear voice rang out from the rear of the cathedral, "You're all a bunch of wankers." The message was repeated several times as protocol officers escorted him from the cathedral. The Archbishop did not miss a beat in the delivery of his sermon.

I subsequently apologised to the cathedral authorities for the disturbance but found them not concerned. "Oh, you mean Peter," they said, "we know him well. He has lots of messages like that but he usually comes to evening service."

THE DIPLOMATIC AND CONSULAR CORPS

There is often confusion over the differences between diplomatic and consular representatives in Australia. They are both representatives of the governments of their home countries but they do have different status and responsibilities.

The Diplomatic Corps

A diplomatic mission represents its country in Australia. This includes protecting their interests and their nationals in Australia within the limits permitted by international law. They conduct negotiations with Australia. They observe and ascertain by all lawful means the conditions and developments within Australia and report these to their home government. They promote friendly relations between their country and Australia and develop economic, cultural and scientific relations.

The head of a diplomatic mission is an Ambassador or a High Commissioner. The difference is purely in name. Missions from Commonwealth countries are headed by a High Commissioner and other countries are headed by an Ambassador.

All resident diplomatic missions are located in Canberra as it is the national capital and the seat of the Australian Government. There are about 70 nations represented. Some countries have diplomatic relations with Australia, but their Ambassador is not resident in Australia as they have multiple responsibilities. Indonesia, China and Japan are common locations for non-resident diplomatic missions and there are about 20 of them.

Australia follows an international agreement called the Vienna Convention which sets out the responsibilities of both the sending and receiving countries in regards to diplomatic missions. These include some special concessions to the visiting diplomats, generally known as diplomatic immunities. These are designed to allow the diplomats to carry out their duties without undue hindrance. Australia recognises these, but they are generally designed to allow diplomats to work in countries with a less democratic base than Australia.

The Consular Corps

A consular mission protects its citizens and bodies corporate within its jurisdiction in Australia as permitted by international law. It furthers commercial, economic, cultural and scientific relations with Australia. It ascertains by all lawful means the conditions and developments in the commercial, economic, cultural and scientific life in Australia and reports to its home government on these matters and also makes this information available to other interested persons - for example, business people considering establishing a business enterprise in Australia. It helps its citizens and issues passports and travel documents to them, as well as providing visas and other travel advice to Australians. It acts as a notary and civil registrar and performs a wide range of administrative functions for its citizens in Australia - for example, providing assistance on the death of one of its nationals and assisting with any disputes relating to its registered ships and aircraft.

Consular missions are generally located in the capital cities of the States and have specific jurisdictions. Not all countries are represented in all States. For example, a number of consular missions in Melbourne have jurisdiction in Tasmania and South Australia as well as

Victoria. Some diplomatic missions have consular sections and also provide consular functions.

Consular missions may be designated as Consulates-General or as Consulates. The name is a matter of seniority and generally represents the size and importance of the consular mission as decided by the country concerned. Both provide the same services.

Although all diplomatic missions are headed by a national of the country concerned, consular missions may be headed by either a career or an honorary Consul-General or Consul. A career head of post is a national of the country concerned, whereas an honorary head of post is an Australian. Honorary appointments are nominated by the country concerned based on some association with that country which may be business, cultural or perhaps a prior period of residency. Honorary consular missions may offer a limited range of services.

As with diplomatic missions, consular representatives are also granted some concessions based on the Vienna Convention. These are less than those granted to diplomats. Honorary appointments receive less immunities than career appointments.

How Can Diplomatic/Consular Missions Assist Australians?

Apart from issuing visas for travel (although your travel agent will normally do this for you), the missions can be very helpful with background information on the country concerned. Some of the larger missions have very detailed libraries and information services which the public can use.

They are a good starting point for any information on their country and if they cannot provide the information they will normally tell you where it can be found.

If you are hosting a visitor from their country or holding a function which relates to their country, they may be able to offer some help. In the case of a hospitality function, you may consider inviting a consular representative.

For Further Information

- Contact the appropriate protocol office listed in Appendix A.
- For details of diplomatic and consular posts in Australia obtain the publications *Diplomatic List* and *Consular List* from Ausinfo Bookshops listed in Appendix G. These are published twice yearly. For information which is updated daily, consult the website *www.dfat.gov.au/protocol*
- For details of Australian missions overseas (both diplomatic and consular) consult the website *www.dfat.gov.au/missions*
- Capital city white pages directories list most consular missions under the heading 'Consuls'. Diplomatic missions are shown in the Canberra white pages.
- For details on diplomatic and consular privileges consult the two Australian Government Acts of Parliament - *Diplomatic Privileges and Immunities Act 1967* and *Consular Privileges and Immunities Act 1972*. They are available for downloading at *www.lawsearch.gov.au* or copies can be bought from the Ausinfo shops listed in Appendix G.

* * *

During the visit by the Pope in 1986, the motorcade was returning to the Archbishop's residence after a community Mass. As it passed a bus shelter, a figure dressed as the devil, complete with horns and pitchfork, leapt out and ran down the road alongside the cars. This devil was obviously in good physical condition as he kept up the pace for several hundred metres before falling behind.

He had caused no harm (and the Pope had not seen him), but a similar incident had occurred in another capital city and the culprit had been arrested. I asked the police if they intended taking any action. "Let the cost of hiring the outfit be sufficient penalty," was the pragmatic answer.

PATRONAGE

Many organisations like to have a patron. They are not essential but, if the patron is carefully selected and is prepared to be active, they can provide a depth of experience and knowledge which can greatly assist the organisation's executive. The duties of a patron are not clearly defined and the role they play in an organisation can vary greatly depending on the patron's enthusiasm and the organisation's wishes. The role needs to be negotiated. In general terms, the following would be true for all patronages:

- A patron is never part of the executive. A patron has no executive power but their knowledge and experience may have considerable influence in the executive's decision-making process.
- A patron can be influential in gaining support for the organisation from outside bodies and individuals
- Patrons are entitled to be advised of the aspirations, progress and financial viability of the organisation and to offer advice and expertise when requested.
- Patrons generally fulfil the role of the 'wise old owl' (although they do not have to be old!).

The following guidelines may be useful when considering the appointment of a patron and may also assist those who are approached to be a patron:

- If a person accepts a patronage because of their position - for example, as the local Member of Parliament, the patronage lapses when that office is no longer held. It does not automatically pass on to the new incumbent.

- A patron should have a personal interest in the organisation or the activity. Many patrons have a long history of prior involvement in the organisation itself or in a similar field.
- There is a general understanding that patrons will attend at least one major activity of the organisation each year. Most patrons who have a genuine interest in the organisation will attend many more.
- A patron should receive copies of all annual reports and other papers, such as minutes of meetings, as agreed with the organisation's executive. A patron should be invited to all appropriate hospitality functions.
- A potential patron, such as a prominent politician, may have many requests to act as a patron. Not all will be accepted. An offer to become a patron for a defined period of time can be attractive. The minimum would be two years.
- Senior dignitaries, such as Premiers, will generally not accept patronage for individual organisations where there are several such bodies active within their State. The patronage of an umbrella body is much more likely - for example, patronage of the Shady Palms Yacht Club is unlikely as there are dozens of similar yacht clubs, but patronage of the Queensland Yachting Council is a distinct possibility.

Many fund-raising appeals look to have a patron or patrons. In these cases the patrons sought are generally well-known names either in the vice-regal, political or celebrity field. The following guidelines apply here:

- Most fund-raising efforts look to be apolitical and may approach, for example, both the Premier and the Opposition

Leader to be joint patrons. This intention should be made clear at the time the approach is made.

- Patrons are often approached because of their names and positions rather than any special interest in the activity.
- Major fund-raising activities may look at having a Patron-in-Chief with a series of other patrons. For example, a major national appeal may request the Governor-General to be Patron-in-Chief, with the Prime Minister and all the Premiers and Opposition Leaders as patrons. Some may look to adding other well-known business identities and celebrities (whatever they are). There is a limit to the effectiveness of having half your letterhead covered with the names of patrons. As in most things, quality is more important than quantity.
- Some people may be asked to be patrons solely because of their understood ability to attract or raise funds. Experience has shown that this is not always the case. Some people like to see their names in print and are pleased to add the appointment to their personal curriculum vitae while offering very little assistance to the cause.
- If you would like the potential patron to make a donation, this should be stated at the time of the patronage request. It is unfair to have the person accept the patronage and then, some months later, put the 'hard word' on them.
- Patronages for fund-raising activities only last for the period of the appeal.

For Further Information

- Contact the appropriate protocol office listed in Appendix A.

* * *

A group of Australians from an international youth organisation was having morning tea at Government House with the Prince of Wales. The group had gathered early and was quite keyed up for the meeting which was to take place at 10.30. They were still milling around in the reception room at 10.20 and the president was advised to get them organised and brief the group about what was to happen. He eventually established some order and began his briefing. As he was saying, "When the Prince of Wales arrives you should...", a familiar English voice from behind him said, "Too late I am afraid, Mr President. I am already here."

It was a very successful, if informal, meeting.

Appendix A

Australian Protocol Offices

Australian Government

Ceremonial and Hospitality Unit
Department of the Prime Minister and Cabinet
3-5 National Circuit
BARTON ACT 2600
Tel: (02) 6271 5111
Fax: (02) 6271 5976

New South Wales

Office of Protocol
Premier's Department
Level 41
Governor Macquarie Tower
1 Farrer Place
SYDNEY NSW 2000
Tel: (02) 9228 4513
Fax: (02) 9228 5478

Victoria

Protocol and Special Events Branch
Department of Premier and Cabinet
1 Treasury Place
MELBOURNE VIC 3000
Tel: (03) 9651 5126
Fax: (03) 9651 5360

Queensland

Protocol Queensland
Department of the Premier and Cabinet
PO Box 185
BRISBANE ALBERT STREET QLD 4002
Tel: (07) 3224 5921
Fax: (07) 3224 6502
protocol@premiers.qld.gov.au

South Australia

Protocol Unit
Department of the Premier and Cabinet
GPO Box 2343
ADELAIDE SA 5001
Tel: (08) 8226 3631
Fax: (08) 8226 4040

Western Australia

Protocol Branch
Ministry of the Premier and Cabinet
197 St George's Terrace
PERTH WA 6000
Tel: (08) 9222 9888
Fax: (08) 9222 9875

Tasmania

Protocol Office
Executive Division
Department of Premier and Cabinet
GPO Box 123B
HOBART TAS 7001
Tel: (03) 6233 6789
Fax: (03) 6233 3345

Northern Territory

Protocol Branch
Department of the Chief Minister
PO Box 4396
DARWIN NT 0801
Tel: (08) 8999 6238
Fax: (08) 8999 6753

Australian Capital Territory

Government Support Unit
Chief Minister's Department
Level 5 Nara Centre
London Circuit
CANBERRA ACT 2601
Tel: (02) 6205 0192
Fax: (02) 6205 0157

Appendix B

Visiting Dignitary Check List

BASIC INFORMATION

Visitor name and title
Spouse name and title
Date of visit
Contact details for people associated with the visit - Telephone/fax/e-mail

ACTION CHECK LIST ON FIRST NOTIFICATION OF VISIT

Identify one person to be the overall coordinator of the visit project.

Whom do I need to alert to the visit? Chairman/Board/General Manager/Division Heads/Security Officer/Transport Officer/Public Affairs Officer/other organisations who may be included or have an interest in the programme - eg, the appropriate consulate in the case of a senior overseas visitor.

Why is the visitor coming? What are his/her aims? What outcomes is the visitor seeking?

Why have we invited him/her? What are our aims? What outcomes do we want to achieve?

Is there any other external group/organisation/person who has an aim to be achieved? Do we have to give them consideration? How much?

Prepare an outline programme, even if it only contains arrival and departure times at this stage. Update/expand continually.

Will the visitor be accompanied by staff? How many? What are their roles? Will separate programmes be required? Will the numbers of accompanying staff have an impact on proposed engagements, especially hospitality functions?

Will any accompanying spouse require a separate programme?

Does the visitor have a national security profile? Will Federal/State police be involved?

Has the dignitary visited before? Check the previous programme.

Where should the party be accommodated? Is there any known preference? Are we responsible for accommodation? Protect accommodation at an appropriate venue that makes sense in the context of the draft programme. Perhaps initially protect accommodation at more than one hotel.

Review travel times against engagement times (Don't travel for two hours for a 20-minute engagement)

Do any engagements require special dress or are all in business attire?

Determine who will be responsible for particular engagements/elements of the programme.

Request biographical notes (CVs) on the travelling individuals and any appropriate country briefing/background notes.

Will the visitor be accompanied by news media representatives? If so, how many and from what disciplines. Will a news media background information kit be required? Should we invite local media representatives to cover all or some elements of the visit? Is a separate media escort officer/planning officer required?

At each major stage of programme development, send progressive drafts to all persons involved for advice/comment/information. This should include the visitor but they would not necessarily receive all drafts - only at major development stages.

PROGRAMME DEVELOPMENT - OTHER CONSIDERATIONS

Does the visitor and all members of the party speak English? What are the interpreter arrangements?

Are there any special medical restrictions/arrangements? Will a personal physician accompany visitor?

Are gifts to be exchanged? What form of gifts is proposed? What general value? Have they been presented with a gift previously?

Will there be an advance party? When will they visit? What is their composition?

Are there any known special interests by the visitor or spouse? Such interests could be a guide for any leisure time engagements in the programme?

Any restrictions on colours, or other special or religious customs?

If a holy day falls during the visit dates, does the visitor wish to attend worship?

Any preferences/restrictions on formal speeches/responses?

Is there any special flag which should be flown? Should the visitor's national flag be flown/displayed?

Are there any dietary restrictions/dislikes?

Does the visitor drink alcohol? If not, is there an objection to alcohol being served to others at a hospitality function?

Road travel preferences? If there is a large party, is a VIP coach acceptable?

Will the visitor be accompanied by any personal security officers? If so, the appropriate Australian police force must be advised.

Are there any restrictions on news media coverage?

Is a news media conference required? If so, is it a general media call or only specialised media? Who will make the arrangements?

Will a press release be issued before the visit? Will there be a post-visit press release?

Would the visitor be agreeable to 'one-on-one' media interviews if these are requested?

Prepare draft speeches for the host for particular engagements in the programme, if applicable.

Prepare a special page for the host's official visitors' book, if appropriate.

Prepare a special gift card, if appropriate.

Arrange an official photographer.

Test drive routes under the same conditions that are likely to apply on the day of the visit.

Confirm hotel accommodation and transport bookings.

Consider a wet-weather programme.

RECONNAISSANCE/REHEARSAL

If the visit is of any significance, at least one reconnaissance/rehearsal is always necessary. If the visitor is sending an advance party, it is best to have a reconnaissance/rehearsal some time before their visit so that you can show them a firm, workable proposal which they can endorse. It is easier to change a plan than to formulate one under pressure.

Involve the widest possible practicable representation in your reconnaissance party so that all involved in the planning can see/hear the concerns and plans of others.

Prepare a detailed reconnaissance programme. Send to all who should be involved, even though some people may not be able to attend on the day.

At a venue, avoid sitting in a conference room discussing the visit. Always try to do it 'on site', solving problems and answering questions as you walk.

Determine the composition and names of the greeting and farewelling parties for each venue.

Determine each venue host/escort officer.

Special car entry/parking arrangements.

Crowd control measures.

If there is to be a speech or address is a dais, lectern and suitable public address system available? If there is to be a dais, what are the seating arrangements on the dais? Who is preparing the speech notes for the host and suggested response notes for the visitor?

Is a plaque to be unveiled or similar? Wording on the plaque? General arrangements?

Any special security risks?

Are there restrictions on public entry? Control through ticketing, identification badges, invitations, magnetometer?

Playing of fanfare/musical salute/national anthems required. Band/tape/CD? Who is responsible?

Any other ceremonial/entertainment considerations?

Restrictions on news media access?

Appointment of a venue media coordinator? Locations for the media? Media riser needed for TV/photographers? Audio splitter box?

Any internal vehicle movements proposed? Who provides the vehicle(s)? What are the seating arrangements?

Does the venue propose the signing of a venue visitors' book?

Is a presentation item proposed? If so, what is it? When will it be presented? Does it clash with the overall host's gift?

Dress proposals? Is a change into protective clothing or the wearing of protective equipment necessary? Has the visitor agreed to this?

What are the emergency medical arrangements?

Are the timings for each segment of the visit realistic?

If elevators are to be used, is there sufficient capacity for the size of the party? Will the elevator(s) be dedicated with a driver? What is the procedure/reaction time in the event of a mechanical problem?

If stairways are used, are they suitable in terms of width, tread surface and steepness?

Is the venue to be in 'working' or 'inspection' order?

Does the proposed programme appear to flow sensibly? Are there any awkward or contrived activities?

Collect additional biographical and background notes/briefing literature on each of the venues visited and the hosts at each venue if these are appropriate.

Collect telephone numbers for use on the day of the visit (fixed and mobile).

Collect any sketch plans/layouts and so on if these could assist in the visitor briefing papers or programme format.

Following the reconnaissance/rehearsal, update the draft programme and redistribute to all concerned.

FINAL PREPARATIONS

Obtain final approval for the programme, print and distribute.

Consider welcoming gift/message/briefing kit to place in hotel rooms

Final checks with venue hosts.

GOOD LUCK!

Appendix C

Hospitality Check List

BASIC INFORMATION

Date and time of the function - luncheon, dinner or cocktail reception.

Name of the host.

Purpose of the function.

Contact names and details, ie, venue coordinator/caterer/guest of honour contact.

INITIAL PREPARATIONS

Determine budget.

Determine the number of guests.

Confirm availability of preferred venue(s) Make a tentative booking.

Book a caterer (if catering does not come with the venue).

Prepare a draft running sheet.

Prepare a list of guest categories and numbers of guests in each.

Gather appropriate background and biographical notes.

Confirm the outline arrangements with the host.

DETAILED PREPARATIONS

Develop the guest list with names and addresses.

Discuss the menu with the caterer.

Determine whether a gift/memento item will be required.

Reconnaissance visit to the venue. Matters to be checked include:

- The name and contact details of the person from the venue who will be your contact at the function.
- Availability of guest parking.
- Access to the function room. Is a map required?
- Availability of a suitable table in the foyer for name cards etc.
- Availability of a cloak room or other arrangements.
- Signage to guide guests.
- Room layout.
- Room decoration and napery colour scheme.
- Availability of a lectern and a dais.
- Suitable audio system, including the ability to play tapes/CD should an anthem be required.
- Arrangements for interpreters.

- Lighting on the lectern/dais.
- Security arrangements.
- Facilities for any ceremonial activities.
- News media access and location. Refreshments for the media.
- Staff refreshments and location for storing gifts/mementos etc.

On return from the reconnaissance, update the draft running sheet.

Print invitation cards, reply slips and any administrative instructions/maps.

Dispatch invitations.

Preparation of draft speeches.

Print menus.

Confirm the developing arrangements with the host.

ONE WEEK BEFORE THE FUNCTION

Consolidate the guest list and follow up any guests who have not replied by telephone, if appropriate.

Prepare a draft seating plan.

Prepare name/table cards.

Prepare a seating plan.

Finalise the running sheet and distribute to all involved.

Confirm all arrangements with the venue operator and caterer.

ON THE DAY OF THE FUNCTION

Arrive in good time at the venue. Walk the course that the guests will follow.

Talk/walk through the function with the venue supervisor.

Check cleanliness of the rest rooms.

Brief staff and layout name/table cards.

Appendix D

Formal Replies to Invitations

Acceptance

>
> Mr and Mrs John Brown
> have the honour to accept the invitation of
> His Excellency the Governor and Mrs Smith
> to attend a Dinner (or evening reception or other occasion)
> on Monday December 1, 2001, at 7.30 pm
>
>
> The Invitations Officer
> Government House
> MELBOURNE VIC 3004   14 November 2001

Decline

Mr and Mrs John Brown
have the honour to receive the invitation of
His Excellency the Governor and Mrs Smith
to attend a Dinner (or evening reception or other occasion)
on Monday December 1, 2001, at 7.30 pm
but regret that they will be unable to attend
as they will be interstate.*

The Invitations Officer
Government House
MELBOURNE VIC 3004   14 November 2001

Reason for declining

Appendix E

Forms of Address

GENERAL EXAMPLES OF ADDRESSING TITLED AND OFFICIAL PERSONS

(NOT NECESSARILY LISTED IN ORDER OF PRECEDENCE)

TITLE	HOW REFERRED TO	SALUTATION IN CORRESPONDENCE	HOW ADDRESSED
The Queen	Her Majesty The Queen	Your Majesty	First and last meeting each day - "Your Majesty" otherwise "Ma'am"
A Royal Duke	His Royal Highness The Duke of	Your Royal Highness	First and last meeting each day - "Your Royal Highness" otherwise "Sir"

Forms of Address

A Prince	His Royal Highness (The) Prince	Your Royal Highness	First and last meeting each day - "Your Royal Highness" otherwise "Sir"
A Princess	Her Royal Highness (The) Princess..........	Your Royal Highness	First and last meeting each day - "Your Royal Highness" otherwise "Ma'am"
Governor-General*	His Excellency the Governor-General *or* His Excellency Sir/Mr................	Your Excellency	"Your Excellency" or "Sir"
Wife of the Governor-General*	Her Excellency Lady........or Her Excellency Mrs..........	Your Excellency	"Your Excellency" or "Ma'am"
Governor of State*	His/Her Excellency The Governor *or* His/Her Excellency Sir/Dame/Mr/Mrs....	Your Excellency	First and last meeting each day - "Your Excellency" otherwise "Sir" or "Ma'am"

On presentation to the persons listed above, it was traditional for gentlemen to bow and for ladies to curtsy. This is no longer the general practice in Australia and is rarely seen, especially with Vice-Regal office holders. Note that the pronunciation of "Ma'am" rhymes with 'Pam' and NOT 'Palm'.

* Some holders of Vice-Regal office have indicated that they prefer not to use the title "Your Excellency", especially when addressed in conversation. The less formal method of address would be "Governor-General" or "Governor"

TITLE	HOW REFERRED TO	SALUTATION IN CORRESPONDENCE	HOW ADDRESSED
Wife of State Governor	Lady...... or Mrs.......	Dear Lady ....or Mrs.....	No title as wife of Governor, and not "Your Excellency". Use private title only.
Duke	The Duke of............	Dear Duke	"Your Grace" or "Duke"
Duchess	The Duchess of	Dear Duchess	"Your Grace" or "Duchess"
Marquess	The Marquess of......	Dear Lord..................	Lord......................
Marchioness	The Marchioness of...............	Dear Lady.................	Lady.....................
Earl	The Earl of...................	Dear Lord..............	Lord.........................
Countess	The Countess of.............	Dear Lady..............	Lady........................
Viscount	The Viscount..........	Dear Lord..............	Lord.........................
Viscountess	The Viscountess of...........	Dear Lady..............	Lady........................
Baron	Lord.......................	Dear Lord..............	Lord.........................
Baroness	Lady......................	Dear Lady..............	Lady........................
Baronet	Sir John Brown	Dear Sir John	Sir John
Wife of Baronet	Lady Brown	Dear Lady Brown	Lady Brown
Knight	Sir Frederick Brown	Dear Sir Frederick	Sir Frederick
Wife of Knight	Lady Brown	Dear Lady Brown	Lady Brown

Forms of Address

Prime Minister	The Prime Minister	Dear Prime Minister	Prime Minister or "Sir" or "Mr/Mrs/Ms................"
Premier of State	The Premier	Dear Premier	Premier or "Sir" or "Mr/Mrs/Ms............"
Minister of the Crown Federal or State	The Minister for/of.....................	Dear Minister	Minister or "Sir" or "Mr/Mrs/Ms............"
Judge of the High or Supreme Court	The Honourable (Mr) Justice..........	Dear Justice	"Your Honour" or "Sir" or "Judge........."
Judge of the Federal or Industrial Relations Court	The Honourable (Mr.) Justice.........	Dear Judge	"Your Honour" or "Sir" or "Judge......."
Judge of the County Court	His/Her Honour Judge......	Dear Judge	"Your Honour" or "Judge ......"
Ambassador	His/Her Excellency the Ambassador of..............	Your Excellency	"Your Excellency", "Mr/Madam Ambassador"
High Commissioner	His/Her Excellency the High Commissioner for............	Your Excellency	"Your Excellency", "Mr/Madam High Commissioner"
Career Consuls-General	The Consul-General of........	Dear Consul-General	"Consul-General" or "Mr/Mrs/Ms."
Honorary Consuls-General	The Consul-General for.......	Dear Consul-General	"Consul-General" or "Mr/Mrs/Ms."
Career Consuls	The Consul of..................	Dear Consul	"Consul" or "Mr/Mrs/Ms."
Honorary Consuls	The Consul for..................	Dear Consul	"Consul" or "Mr/Mrs/Ms."

Archbishop	<u>Church of England</u> The Most Reverend the Archbishop of Melbourne	Dear Archbishop	"Your Grace"
	<u>Roman Catholic</u> The Most Reverend the Archbishop of Melbourne	My Lord Archbishop	"Your Grace"
Bishop	<u>Church of England</u> The Right Reverend the Bishop of............	Dear Bishop	"Bishop................."
	<u>Roman Catholic</u> The Most Reverend...............	My Lord	"My Lord"
Dean	<u>Church of England</u> The Very Reverend the Dean of............	Dear Dean	"Dean Jones" or "Dean"
Lord Mayor	** The Right Honourable The Lord Mayor of	Dear Lord Mayor	" Lord Mayor"
Wife of Lord Mayor	The Lady Mayoress of	Dear Lady Mayoress	" Lady Mayoress"
Mayor, if a man	The Mayor of...............	Dear Mr. Mayor	"Mr Mayor" or "Sir"
Wife of Mayor	The Mayoress	Dear Madam Mayoress	"Mayoress" or "Mrs. Smith"
Mayor, if a woman	The Mayor of...............	Dear Madam Mayor	"Madam Mayor"
Husband of a Mayor	Mr.................	Dear Mr.................	"Mr......................"

| Municipal Councillor | Councillor............ | Dear Councillor | "Councillor Jones" |

** Note that the Lord Mayor of Darwin is referred to as The Right Worshipful the Lord Mayor of Darwin.

Appendix F

Official Commonwealth And State Symbols

Official Commonwealth And State Symbols

	AUSTRALIA	NEW SOUTH WALES	VICTORIA	QUEENSLAND	SOUTH AUSTRALIA	WESTERN AUSTRALIA	TASMANIA	AUSTRALIAN CAPITAL TERRITORY	NORTHERN TERRITORY
Coat of Arms	Yes	Yes	Yes	Yes	Yes	Yes	Yes	Yes (Canberra)	Yes
Flag	Yes	Yes	Yes	Yes	Yes	Yes	Yes	Yes	Yes
Badge	No	Yes	Yes	Yes	Yes	Yes	Yes	No	No
Anthem	Yes	No	No	No	No	No	No	No	No
Floral Emblem	Golden Wattle	Waratah	Common Pink Heath	Cooktown Orchid	Sturts Desert Pea	Red and Green Kangaroo Paw	Tasmanian Blue Gum	Royal Bluebell	Sturts Desert Rose
Faunal Emblem 1	No	Kookaburra	Helmeted Honeyeater	Koala	Hairy Nosed Wombat	Numbat	No	Gang-gang Cockatoo	Wedge-tailed Eagle
Faunal Emblem 2	No	Platypus	Leadbeater's Possum	Brolga	No	Black Swan	No	No	Red Kangaroo
Fish/Fossil Emblem	No	Eastern Blue Groper	No	No	No	Gogo Fish	No	No	No
Gemstone Emblem	Opal	No	No	Sapphire Blue Ice	Opal Desert Fire	No	Crocoite	No	No
Colours	Green/Gold	Silver/Blue	Blue/Silver	No official colours. Maroon/white or gold.	Red/Blue/Gold	Black/Gold	No	Blue/Yellow	Black/Silver/Ochre

Appendix G

Australian Government Information Shops

The locations and contact numbers for Australian Government Information Shops trading as AUSINFO are shown below. AUSINFO was formerly known as the Australian Government Publishing Service.

Adelaide   60 Weymouth Street   Tel: (08) 8231 0144
                 Adelaide SA 5000   Fax: (08) 8231 0135

Australian Government Information Shops

Brisbane	City Plaza Cnr Adelaide and George Sts Brisbane QLD 4000	Tel: (07) 3229 6822 Fax: (07) 3229 1387
Canberra	10 Mort Street Canberra ACT 2600	Tel: (02) 6247 7211 Fax: (02) 6257 1797
Darwin	NT Government Publications 13 Smith Street Darwin NT 5790	Tel: (08) 8999 7152 Fax: (08) 8999 7972
Hobart	31 Criterion Street Hobart TAS 7000	Tel: (03) 6234 1403 Fax: (03) 6234 1364
Melbourne	190 Queen Street Melbourne VIC 3000	Tel: (03) 9670 4224 Fax: (03) 9670 4115
Perth	469 Wellington Street Perth WA 6000	Tel: (08) 9322 4737 Fax: (08) 9481 4412
Sydney	32 York Street Sydney NSW 2000	Tel: (02) 9299 6737 Fax: (02) 9262 1219
Townsville	277 Flinders Mall Townsville QLD 4810 Freecall: 1800 805 896	Tel: (07) 4721 5212 Fax: (07) 4721 5217
For Mail Order Sales	GPO Box 84 Canberra ACT 2601	
For Phone Orders	Tel: 13 24 47	

Appendix H

Australian National Anthem

Australians all let us rejoice,
For we are young and free;
We've golden soil and wealth for toil;
Our home is girt by sea;
Our land abounds in nature's gifts
Of beauty rich and rare;
In history's page, let every stage
Advance Australia Fair.
In joyful strains then let us sing,
Advance Australia Fair.

Beneath our radiant Southern Cross
We'll toil with hearts and hands;
To make this Commonwealth of ours
Renowned of all the lands;
For those who've come across the seas
We've boundless plains to share;
With courage let us all combine
To Advance Australia Fair
In joyful strains then let us sing,
Advance Australia Fair.